Restored

Reawakening the soul's true essence

James Ogunnusi

Acknowledgements

With a heart filled with profound gratitude, I begin by offering my thanks to God Almighty for His abundant grace, which has enabled me to complete this book. His divine inspiration and insight have been the driving force behind this endeavour. I am deeply grateful for the gift of good health and the abundance of support and resources with which He has blessed me.

To my dear parents, Surveyor, Pastor Michael Bolanle Ogunnusi, and Rebecca Ajibola Ogunnusi, I extend my sincere appreciation for your unwavering love, care, and prayers throughout the years. Your godly investment in me has nurtured a deep love for God within my heart. Your guidance has illuminated the path, as you exemplified the scripture that says, "train up a child in the way he should go, and when he is old, he will not depart from it." I am forever indebted to you for the legacy of faith you have bestowed upon me.

My gratitude extends to my one and only sister, Dr. Bunmi Kotun (nee: Ogunnusi), for her incredible support and invaluable contribution to this book. Her meticulous proofreading and valuable feedback have enhanced the quality of this work.

I offer special thanks to Pastors Clement & Rebecca Bamgbade for their hospitality and unwavering support upon my return to the UK. Your investment in my educational development and guidance have played a significant role in shaping the person I am today. Your fatherly and motherly care, along with your prayers and support, will forever be etched in my memory.

To my best friend, lover, heartthrob, and the most understanding wife in the world, I express a massive thank you. Your sacrifice and unwavering support have been the cornerstone of this book's completion. You selflessly took on various responsibilities in our home, allowing me ample time to dedicate to this project. You are a rare gem, unmatched in your love and dedication. From the depths of my heart, I love you beyond words. I am equally grateful for your loving and caring motherhood, as you have been a blessing to our blessed, beautiful, and God-fearing daughter, Michelle. To Michelle, my darling daughter, I extend my gratitude for your understanding and patience, as you sacrificed numerous daddy-daughter playdates to support me in completing this book.

I wish to express my heartfelt appreciation to my mother-in-law, Mrs. Helen Erekpaine, and my Father-in-law, Tiere Johnson Erekpaine, for their unwavering support, love, and prayers. You raised a godfearing daughter whom I am proud to call my wife. My gratitude also goes to my wife's siblings, Rhoma, Fene, Serorie & Bro Dijila, for their support and contributions in raising my wife and warmly welcoming me into the family as a son-in-law.

To the co-editors, proofreaders, and contributors, I am sincerely thankful for the time and effort you dedicated to refining this book. Your valuable insights, feedback, and fresh perspectives have elevated this work to its highest potential. A special mention goes to Sotonye Deru, Dr. Bunmi Kotun, Yemi Babafunso, Sade Osundosumu, Oladunni Ikumelo, Isobel Egbarin, Vanessa Rose, Sarah Mbadiwe, Oriade Adenuga, Simbo Okolo, and Pastors Ishola & Doris Familusi.

Speaking of whom, I would like to extend my special appreciation to Pastors Ishola & Doris Familusi for their spiritual oversight and providing a platform for my spiritual growth and the flourishing of my God-given gifts. Your unwavering support, prayers, and daily spiritual investments have been invaluable. I am also deeply grateful for your belief in me, and the foreword you graciously provided for the book.

To my dear friend who is closer than a brother, Pastor David & Lady Beatrice Oluwatayo, and their lovely daughter Apphia Oluwatayo, I extend my love and appreciation for your unwavering presence and support.

Finally, I extend my heartfelt gratitude to the numerous spiritual leaders who have impacted my life through prayers, teachings, mentoring, preaching, and counselling. Your spiritual and physical investment has been instrumental in shaping my journey, and I am forever indebted to you all.

In conclusion, I am deeply thankful to all who have played a significant role in making this book a reality. Your support, love, and prayers have been the bedrock of my inspiration and success. May God bless each of you abundantly.

Copyright © 2023 by James Ogunnusi

All rights reserved.

All rights reserved. Printed in the United Kingdom. No part of this book may be reproduced, stored in a retrieval system, or transmitted, in any form or by any means, electronic, mechanical, photocopying, recording, or otherwise, without the prior written permission of the publisher or author, except in the case of brief quotations embodied in critical reviews and certain other non-commercial uses permitted by copyright law.

For information contact; jamsola2002@yahoo.com

Contents

Foreword	IX
Introduction	XI
1. The Gap Theory	1
2. Restoration of Order	6
3. In the Image of God	10
4. The Flesh, The World and The Devil	21
5. The Fall and Death of the Living Soul	28
6. The Corrupted Soul and God's Displeasure	34
7. The Law as a Schoolmaster	43
8. Jesus Christ: The Restorer of the Living Soul	50
9. The Rebirth of the Living Soul	60
10. Bearing the Image of Adam	68
11. Identifying with Christ's Sufferings	84
12. Our Spirituality	87
13. Our Active Engagement in the Growth Process	106
14. The Hope of Eternity	118

Study Guides

Foreword

James Ogunnusi has been known to me for several years now, and I have come to respect him as a man of integrity whose passion for God is unmatched. He is currently serving on board the leadership team at Rock Church based in Rochester, Kent, United Kingdom, as an associate pastor.

His selfless service, commitment, and dedication to God is deeply admirable, and it is with great excitement that I write the foreword for his first book.

RESTORED is a book filled with such depths and insights that takes the reader on a journey that clearly reveals the original thoughts and plan of God for man, the fall of man from grace, the consequences and impact of this fall, and God's divine intervention through His Son, Jesus Christ, which has opened the pathway of man's restoration to that original plan and purpose of God.

The author has carefully, in a revelatory pattern, interconnected scriptures from both the Old and New Testaments to take the reader on this journey of discovery, making this book an eye-opening wealth of both spiritual and practical knowledge. It is able to transform lives and deepen one's faith as a child of God.

As you read this book, whether you are searching for answers to what life is really all about, a new believer or a mature Christian, I believe you will come to a place of conviction, knowing that God has indeed made a way to be truly delivered from the calamity of the Adamic sin nature and be restored back to

Him. As a result, we are now able to live out God's original intent and purpose for mankind right here on earth.

Much blessings!

Ishola Familusi
Senior Pastor,
Rock Church, Rochester UK.

Introduction

Are you tired of wondering if Christians can truly experience the perfection described in the Bible? Do you long for a thorough understanding of the process that results in genuine transformation? If so, then I invite you to join me on an extraordinary journey of restoration and soul awakening through my book, "Restored: Reawakening the Soul's True Essence."

Individuals must rediscover their true selves and experience the profound restoration that can only be found through a deep connection with God in this modern age. The issue is that many people have lost sight of the importance and urgency of this restoration. Our souls are in desperate need of revival, and the consequences go far beyond our personal lives—they affect the very fabric of the Church.

I have crafted a compelling narrative that unravels the mysteries of spiritual restoration through meticulous research, personal experiences, and divine revelations. This book offers profound insights into the biblical journey, beginning with the world before man's existence, the tragic fall from grace, and the subsequent restoration of order.

However, this is more than just a retelling of old stories; it is a road map for your own personal transformation. With each chapter, I will walk you through the stages of development required to live a life free of the bonds of sin and its destructive urges. You will discover your true essence—your divine image as created by God.

Allow me to demonstrate how Jesus Christ, the Last Adam, has come to reconcile us to our original essence. Understanding the significance of Christ's sufferings and embracing our spirituality allows us to actively participate in the growth process and experience a profound reawakening of our souls.

The urgency of this restoration cannot be overstated. If we fail to recognize its significance, we risk undermining the Church's power and effectiveness. The world requires fully restored Christians who are walking in their true essence. Only then will we be able to effect the transformative change that our world so desperately requires.

"Restored: Reawakening the Soul's True Essence" is more than just a book; it is a catalyst for personal revival and spiritual transformation. It will enable you to embrace your divine identity, comprehend the importance of restoration, and ignite a flame within you that will burn brightly for all to see.

Don't be satisfied with a mediocre life. Take hold of the profound truths contained within these pages and live a life filled with true purpose, joy, and freedom. Your soul's restoration is waiting for you, and this book will help you get there. Are you ready to embark on a remarkable personal transformation journey? Then explore "Restored" to learn about the power of awakening your soul's true essence.

Chapter 1

The Gap Theory

In our quest to understand the mysteries of creation and the age of the Earth, we delve into the discoveries made by archaeologists and the accuracy of carbon dating technology. This scientific method allows us to determine the age of bones with remarkable precision (Job 12:8). However, when we consider dinosaur bones that predate the existence of humans, we are faced with a perplexing question: if the Earth is believed to be only 6,000 years old, how do we account for these ancient fossils? This suggests that creation and existence extend beyond the 6,000-year timeframe commonly associated with human history (Psalm 90:2).

The age of the oldest dinosaur fossils excavated by humans indicates that these colossal creatures lived on Earth long before the first man, Adam, was created. With the advancement of technology, Scientists now estimate the earth to be 4.54 billion years old. Such a realisation leads us to ponder the existence of nations before Adam. If these massive animals roamed the Earth, it is logical to assume that the nations preceding Adam must have been a nation of angels, as it was angels who joined the rebellion with Lucifer against God. If the nations were then composed of angels, it is important to note that Angels can transform into terrestrial or celestial beings. So while on earth, it can be assumed they lived here as terrestrial beings.

A glimpse into the possibility of the physical size of the population of the nations before Adam can be found in Genesis 6:4, where giants populated the earth after angels (sons of God) had intercourse with the daughters of men. This indicates the physical proportion of an angel, hence why angels tend to tell men when they appear to them, "Fear Not", because their size could possibly be intimidating. Animals are generally proportionate to humans in size, so just as humans today are proportional to most animals, including those larger in size, the nations before Adam would have been in proportion to the gigantic creatures that inhabited the Earth during that era.

In Isaiah chapter 14, we encounter a passage that addresses Lucifer, also known as the morning star. Isaiah describes Lucifer as the shining one and the son of the morning (Isaiah 14:12). The name Lucifer itself signifies the shining one, and he is referred to as a son, specifically the son of the morning. This biblical depiction highlights the significance of Lucifer and invites us to explore further.

Isaiah continues to recount how Lucifer, having been cut down to the ground, weakened nations (Isaiah 14:12–17). It becomes clear that one of his crimes leading to his downfall was the act of weakening nations. The passage suggests that nations existed before Lucifer's fall and that his actions had the power to weaken them. Lucifer deceived these nations, presenting himself as their messiah, and sought to establish an empire. He relied on the support of his subjects, whom he was meant to protect as a covering cherub, but they joined him in his quest to establish a parallel kingdom.

These insights from Scripture open the door to deeper contemplation. The preacher in Ecclesiastes reminds us that there is nothing new under the sun and that what has been in ancient times before us will be again (Ecclesiastes 1:9–10). This prompts us to explore the Gap Theory, a concept that sheds light on the state of the Earth prior to the creation of humankind.

Genesis 1:1 declares, "In the beginning, God created the heavens and the earth." This foundational verse confirms the goodness and perfection of God's creative work. However, Genesis 1:2 presents a puzzling description of the Earth as being without form, void, and covered in darkness. This raises questions about the Earth's initial condition and its origins.

Scriptural insights guide our understanding of these verses. The absence of darkness in God, as affirmed in 1 John 1:5, suggests that darkness could not have originated from God's creation. Furthermore, passages like Isaiah 66:1 and Acts 7:49 portray heaven and earth as complementary entities. If darkness has no place in heaven, it follows that darkness would not have been present in God's initial creation.

The book of Revelation offers additional glimpses into the nature of heaven, describing it as a place where the glory of God illuminates everything, rendering the sun and moon unnecessary (Revelation 21:23; 22:5). These verses further reinforce the notion that darkness has no place in God's perfect creation.

To make sense of the transition from a perfect creation to a state of formlessness and voidness, proponents of the Gap Theory propose the occurrence of a catastrophic event between Genesis 1:1 and 1:2. This event, potentially connected to the fall of Satan, is believed to have resulted in the ruin of the Earth, followed by its renewal. Analogies are drawn between this theory and scientific concepts such as the big bang, suggesting a significant event leading to the formation of our current world.

However, it is crucial to acknowledge that the Gap Theory remains speculative, as the Bible does not explicitly outline a gap between Genesis 1:1 and 1:2. Critics argue that the creation account can be understood as a continuous narrative without necessitating a gap. They propose that the formlessness and voidness described in Genesis 1:2 represent a state before God's creative actions brought order and beauty to the Earth.

While the Gap Theory offers an intriguing perspective on the creation account, we approach this topic with an open mind, recognising that the ultimate understanding of creation lies in God's sovereign knowledge and revelation (Job 38:4). As believers, our focus should centre on the central message of the Bible: God's creative power, His redemptive plan through Jesus Christ, and our response to His grace and love. While the Gap Theory provides an interesting exploration of creation, it should not overshadow the foundational teachings and essential truths of Scripture.

Understanding the Gap Theory enriches our comprehension of the Earth's origins, our place within God's grand design, and the significance of His redemption plan. It invites us to ponder the mysteries of creation while acknowledging that the ultimate truth and meaning lie in God's divine wisdom and revelation.

***

Lucifer's Fall and Rebellion

God, in His grand design, created the heavens as His majestic throne and the earth as His humble footstool (Isaiah 66:1; Acts 7:49). These symbolic representations highlight the greatness of God, emphasising that even the vast expanse of heaven cannot contain His glory. Before the creation of the heavens and the earth, God existed, and His position remained unchanged. The Psalms repeatedly testify to His lofty dwelling place above the heavens (Psalm 8:1; 50:4; 57:5; 11). Therefore, heaven was not created as a dwelling place for God, nor was the earth.

When God populated heaven, He appointed angels to serve in various capacities. Among them, He placed an archangel named Lucifer in Eden, entrusting him with the governance of Earth. This is evident from the existence of Lucifer's own throne. However, pride and rebellion tainted Lucifer's heart, leading to his fall. In Ezekiel 28:12-19, the prophet addresses the King of Tyre, using him as a parallel to depict the spiritual rebellion of Lucifer. The passage describes Lucifer's dwelling in Eden, adorned with precious stones and musical instruments. He was an anointed cherub who covered God's presence and walked amidst fiery stones. Initially, he was perfect in his ways, but iniquity was found in him, giving birth to his rebellion.

This Scripture provides insights into Lucifer's location in Eden and his perfect state before succumbing to pride and rebellion. His sin was not merely a desire to resemble God in appearance, but an aspiration to usurp God's position and authority. It was a coveting of God's throne and a yearning to be worshipped as God Himself. To illustrate this concept, let us consider an analogy. Suppose I am the Prime Minister of the United Kingdom, and while holding this esteemed office, I passionately desire to become the President of the United States, disregarding my loyalty to my country. If I were to rally a faction of the British Parliament and armed forces to wage war against the United States in an attempt to claim the presidency, it would be considered an act of disloyalty and betrayal. The United States, prioritising its national interests, would respond with force to counter such an intrusion.

This snippet illuminates the iniquity of Lucifer, as he desired to abandon his assigned jurisdiction and ascend to overthrow God's authority. His insatiable pride led him to wage war in pursuit of his ambitious desires. Similarly, Isaiah 14:12-14 laments the fall of Lucifer, referred to as the "morning star" or "Day Star." The passage describes how Lucifer, in his pride, sought to ascend to heaven and establish his dominion. However, his rebellion resulted in his downfall, weakening the nations.

The nations mentioned in the context of Lucifer's weakening are representative of the various regions and powers that existed at the time. While specific nations may not be explicitly named, the passage signifies the influence and impact of Lucifer's rebellion on the earthly realm.

These passages reveal the tragic narrative of Lucifer's fall from grace and his desire to exalt himself above God. They provide us with a glimpse into the consequences of pride and rebellion, reminding us of the importance of humility and obedience in our own lives.

Chapter 2

Restoration of Order

In the beginning, God created the heavens and the earth, but a gap occurred, as explained in Chapter 1, resulting in the judgement of Lucifer and his fallen angels. This judgement caused the earth to become formless, void, and flooded with water, and darkness was upon the face of the deep.

To restore order to this chaotic world, the Spirit of God hovered over the face of the waters. Then God spoke, saying, "Let there be light," and there was light. This light, according to John 1:3-5, was Jesus Christ, the light of men. All things were made through Him, and without Him, nothing was made. This light shone in the darkness, and the darkness could not comprehend it. Just as turning on a light in a dark room dissipates the darkness, the light of Christ shining in the darkness disturbed Lucifer and his fallen angels. Having grown accustomed to darkness, they were unable to comprehend the startling brightness of the light. Out of God's mercy, considering their appointed time for final judgement had not yet come, a territory or space was created for them. This aligns with Matthew 8:28, when devils possessed two men and cried out to Jesus, asking if He had come to torment them before the appointed time.

The devil and his angels know there is an everlasting fire prepared for them, as mentioned in Matthew 25:41. However, before their final judgement, some fallen angels and devils are still able to roam freely, relying on the cover of darkness to carry out their evil deeds. Ephesians 6:12 speaks of the rulers of the darkness of this world.

In Matthew 25:31, the devils negotiate with Jesus, asking to be cast into a herd of swine. Jesus grants their request, allowing them to go. In Genesis 1:3-4, I visualize a similar occurrence where, at God's command, the light of Jesus startles the devil and his fallen angels. Though inaudible, their body language and facial expressions silently beg God not to destroy them before their time. God, being a God of principles who acts orderly, looked at the light and saw that it was good. However, to create a place for the devil and his fallen angels to stay, He divided the light from the darkness.

The Light mentioned in verse 3 is Jesus Christ, and it represents a location called Day. Proverbs 18:10 describes the name of the Lord as a strong tower where the righteous find safety. Jesus Himself referred to this when He said in John 16:33, "In Me, you may have peace." Ephesians 2:6 speaks of sitting together in heavenly places in Christ Jesus.

Darkness represents a location called Night. Isaiah 29:15 warns of those who hide their plans in the darkness, thinking no one sees or knows. Ephesians 5:11 urges us not to participate in the unfruitful deeds of darkness but rather expose them. Romans 13:12 declares that the night is almost gone and the day is near. Therefore, we should lay aside the deeds of darkness and put on the armor of light.

Romans 13:12 references both night and day, darkness and light, which aligns with 1 Thessalonians 5:5, stating that believers are children of light and of the day, not of the night or darkness.

Jesus Himself spoke of the need to work while it is day, for the night is coming when no one can work, as mentioned in John 9:4. Although some men work at night, the majority are asleep during that time, while devils and demonic forces are more active. In Matthew 13:25, Jesus said that while men slept, the enemy came and sowed tares among the wheat.

The earth revolving on its axis results in the experience of day and night. However, even during the night season, when darkness and the works of darkness intensify, it is important to note that, as children of God, we are not of darkness because Darkness does not belong to God. 1 John 1:5 affirms that God is light, and in Him, there is no darkness at all. Therefore, as children of light, we have no association with darkness and should not fear the dark or nighttime because God is with us. Psalm 23:4 assures us that even when walking through the valley of the shadow of death, we should fear no evil, for God is with us. Psalm 127:2 states that God gives His beloved sleep.

The activities of devils are heightened in the darkness of night, and their presence and influence are more concentrated. Even in the midst of their operations, we as believers need not be concerned. For in Psalm 91:5, it speaks of the terror that may come by night, likened to a full-scale terrorist attack. It also assures us that during the day, the attacks will be like arrows, causing damage but not on the same catastrophic scale. In the face of this, we find comfort and assurance in the knowledge that God's protection surrounds us. He envelops us in His feathers, providing shelter and security. He provides sustenance and strength even in the midst of darkness and evil around us, like a table set before us in the presence of our enemies. We can take refuge under His wings and find comfort in His unwavering presence if we have unwavering trust.

God continued to restore order to the chaotic state of the world by dividing the waters and forming the sky above. He then caused the remaining water below to gather together in one place so the dry land might appear. This indicates God didn't have to recreate the earth; he was simply restoring order and putting things back in their rightful place. The dry land that appeared was called earth, and the waters he gathered together in one place were called seas. He then spoke to the earth, causing grass, trees, plants, cattle, and beasts of the earth to emerge. Then He spoke to the sky, bringing forth lights. These natural lights differ from the Spiritual Light in Genesis 1:3 that birthed all things into existence. From the waters, God called forth sea creatures and flying birds. All of this occurred within five days.

On the sixth day, after God had fully restored order to the earth, He turned His attention away from calling forth things from the earth and spoke within Himself (to the Trinity), saying, "Let Us make man in Our image, according to Our likeness." Thus, He created man in His own image and likeness. Since God is a Spirit and rules over heaven, to make us like Him, He gave us a domain to rule over—the fish of the sea, the birds of the air, the cattle, all the earth, and every creeping thing that creeps on the earth (Genesis 1:26).

Genesis 1:27 affirms, "So God created man in His own image; in the image of God, He created him; male and female, He created them."

Chapter 3

In the Image of God

The Creation of Adam and the Imprint of God's Image

When God created man in Genesis 1:26, He spoke, saying, "Let Us make man in Our image, according to Our likeness." This reveals that the creation of man occurred in two distinct parts or stages.

In the initial stage of man's creation, God made him in His own image. As stated in Genesis 1:27, "So God created man in His own image." We also learn from John 4:24 that God is a Spirit. Furthermore, in Acts 17:28, Paul affirms that we live, move, and have our being in God, for we are His offspring. According to John 3:6, those born of the Spirit are spirits.

Let us examine Acts 17:28 further. Paul mentioned that in God we live, which aligns with Galatians 5:25, where Paul urges us to live in the Spirit. Paul also said that in God we move, resonating with the exhortation to "walk in the Spirit." Although there is no direct correlation to Galatians 5 regarding our being in Him, we can infer that if our life is in the Spirit and our movements are in the Spirit, then our very existence must also be a spiritual one. As offspring of a God who is Spirit, our nature is undoubtedly spiritual.

If we consider that God created man in His own image, it implies that man was made as a spirit. Man's spirit, existing before physical formation, highlights the eternal nature of his being. So in Genesis 1:27, we see man's spiritual essence, intricately designed and fashioned in the image of God.

In the second part of the creation of man, as described in Genesis 1:26, it mentions being made "according to Our likeness." The word "according" in this context implies a pattern. Although God is a Spirit, He exists as three distinct personalities that are in perfect unity. 1 John 5:7 states, "For there are three that bear record in heaven: the Father, the Word, and the Holy Ghost; and these three are one." This pattern of the three personalities united as one makes God a triune being. If man is to be formed according to this pattern, three entities must be involved, and they must work together as one.

We find compelling evidence in Scripture to support the belief that man first existed as a spirit being before his physical formation and manifestation into the physical world. We can strengthen the case for man's preexistence as a spirit and subsequent formation of body, spirit, and soul by drawing on the wisdom of Jeremiah 1:5 and Psalm 139:13-18.

According to Jeremiah 1:5, God's knowledge and purpose for us precede our physical existence. He knew us before we were born and had already assigned us a unique destiny. This proves that our spirit existed before our physical manifestation.

Psalm 139:13-18 emphasizes God's intimate involvement in our creation even more. He intricately weaves us together in the womb, witnessing our unformed bodies there. This implies that even before we enter the physical realm, God is intimately acquainted with every aspect of our being, including our spirit.

Genesis 2:7 further reveals, "And the Lord God formed man of the dust of the ground and breathed into his nostrils the breath of life, and man became a living soul." In the first part of man's creation, God made man in His own image, indicating that man already existed as a spirit. In the second part, man was formed, signifying the establishment of an order that mirrors the likeness of the Godhead. Thus, we witness the three entities at play during the formation of man: the dust from which his body was created, allowing him to interact physically with the earth; the preexisting spirit introduced into the body through the breath of life (ruach); and the union of the body and spirit giving rise to the third entity—the soul. The soul serves as a medium for interaction between the spirit and the body and encompasses man's emotions, intellect, and will.

The soul came alive as "a Living Soul" and was identified as the essence of man in Genesis 2:7 (KJV) when it states, "Man became a living soul." This living soul serves as the interpreter between the spirit and the body since, as the Scripture affirms, "But the natural man does not receive the things of the Spirit of God, for they are foolishness to him; nor can he know them because they are spiritually discerned" (1 Corinthians 2:14). Therefore, a spirit can communicate with another spirit, but for the body to receive such communication, an interpreter is required—the soul. However, for the soul to fulfill its role as a translator of spiritual matters, it must be alive. John 6:63 states, "It is the Spirit who gives life; the flesh profits nothing." This indicates that the soul came alive through the agency of the Spirit, the breath of life, which bestowed life upon the soul, causing it to become a Living Soul.

***

The Union of Spirit, Body, and Soul

The soul serves as the mediator, receiving from the Spirit and communicating to the body. It is the central point of a man's triune composition. Therefore, although man is referred to as a living soul, he is essentially a spirit who possesses a body that he interacts with through the soul, which is sustained by the spirit. This union of the three entities constitutes the nature of man as a triune being, reflecting the likeness of God, who is also a triune being. Man's composition sets him apart as even the angels do not possess this unique structure.

The unity and oneness within the Godhead find a reflection in man. The Godhead is perfectly synchronized, completely united as one. This mirrors the unity of the body, soul, and spirit that form the composition of man. No human being, surgeon, or doctor knows precisely where the dividing line between these three entities lies—only God does. Regarding Jesus, who is the Word through whom all things were made, Hebrews 4:12 affirms, "For the word of God is quick and powerful, and sharper than any two-edged sword, piercing even to the dividing asunder of soul and spirit." This indicates that only God knows the precise division between the soul and spirit. They are so intertwined that outwardly man appears as one entity, yet he is composed of three entities in perfect unity.

Unlike man, angels are spiritual beings with spiritual bodies, but they possess the ability to transform. Angels can assume human form, and an evil angel can disguise itself as an angel of light. As stated in 2 Corinthians 11:14, "And no marvel; for Satan himself is transformed into an angel of light." This is why we must exercise caution and test the spirits, as stated in 1 John 4:1, "Beloved, believe not every spirit, but try the spirits whether they are of God."

Angels are called ministering spirits in Hebrews 1:14, indicating that they have a mandate to serve us as Christians. Their assignments require them to traverse between heaven and earth. However, earthly or terrestrial bodies cannot enter the heavenly realm, as stated in 1 Corinthians 15:50, "Now this I say, brethren, that flesh and blood cannot inherit the kingdom of God; neither doth corruption inherit incorruption."

Therefore, before man can enter heaven, there must be a transformation of the corrupt human body into an incorruptible spiritual body. This transformation can occur through death, as described in 1 Corinthians 15:42-44, "So also is the resurrection of the dead. It is sown in corruption; it is raised in incorruption. It is sown a natural body; it is raised a spiritual body." Alternatively, the transformation can take place through the rapture. As stated by Paul in 1 Corinthians 15:51-53, "Behold, I show you a mystery; We shall not all sleep (die), but we shall all be changed. In a moment, in the twinkling of an eye, at the last trump: for the trumpet shall sound, and the dead shall be raised incorruptible, and we shall be changed. For this corruptible must put on incorruption, and this mortal must put on immortality."

No spirit has a legal right to operate on earth without a body. God, in His wisdom, has given us physical bodies to carry out His purposes on earth. Demons, on the other hand, seek to possess human bodies in order to carry out their wicked activities.

Angels, being heavenly spiritual beings, are meant to minister to us and assist us on earth. In order to do so legally, they can transform from their celestial bodies to terrestrial bodies. The distinction between celestial bodies and terrestrial bodies is mentioned in 1 Corinthians 15:40. This implies that angels can take on the appearance of humans when they visit us, hence why the Bible encourages us not to forget to show hospitality to strangers, as some have unknowingly entertained angels (Hebrews 13:2).

While Jesus instructed us to cast out demons from the human bodies they've possessed, there is no instruction to cast out angels as they have their own bodies and do not need to possess human bodies. Rather, we are taught to wrestle with spiritual forces. This wrestling is not something we can accomplish in our own strength. Thankfully, we have angels at our disposal whom we can send on assignments to engage in spiritual battles. In the book of Daniel, we see an example of angels wrestling with the princes of Persia at the command of Daniel.

The soul is considered the core or innermost aspect of a person's being. It serves as a bridge between the physical body and the spirit. The soul possesses individuality, consciousness, and personal identity. It encompasses the mind, intellect, emotions, feelings, thoughts, will, reasoning, and more.

The soul became the focal point of human existence because it served as the medium through which the spirit could communicate with and control the body. According to 1 Corinthians 2:14, "But the natural man does not receive the things of the Spirit of God, for they are foolishness to him; nor can he know them because they are spiritually discerned." Thus, the human body requires something to translate or decode spiritual communications into a form that the body can receive and comprehend. However, for the soul to fulfill this role, it must be alive. The "Breath of Life" in man was the Spirit of God, and it is this Spirit that supplies the life through which the soul becomes alive. As stated in John 6:63, "It is the Spirit who gives life; the flesh profits nothing."

**

The Breath of Life: The Spirit's Role in Enlivening the Soul

In accordance with the divine design, the living soul received life from the Spirit. It was a reflection of the Spirit but in a form that the body could comprehend and receive. The soul acted as an intermediary, a translator. It was the vital force that kept the body active and alive. Thus, man bears resemblance to the Godhead, where within the hierarchy of oneness, the Spirit glorifies Jesus (John 16:13-15), and Jesus glorifies the Father (John 12:27-28). Similarly, within the hierarchy of man as a triune being, the Spirit (the breath of life) imparts life to the soul, and the soul imparts life to the body. This interdependency is what makes man uniquely fashioned, a creature directly moulded in the image and likeness of God.

David consistently addressed his soul (Psalm 103:1,2,22; 104:1,35) because the soul was designed to mirror the Spirit, and man is meant to live from his soul, for as a man thinks in his heart, so is he (Proverbs 23:7). Proverbs 4:23 exhorts us to "Keep your heart with all diligence, For out of it spring the issues of life."

Whenever David, the Psalmist, felt discouraged, he understood that it directly reflected the state of his soul. His Spirit-being would then encourage his soul, which, in turn, manifested in David's external countenance. In 1 Samuel 30:6, we read, "Now David was greatly distressed, for the people spoke of stoning him, because the soul of all the people was grieved, every man for his sons and his daughters. But David strengthened himself in the Lord his God."

In times when his soul was distressed, David found his source of strength in the Lord God. The Bible informs us that God is Spirit (John 4:24). Thus, David knew how to turn his soul to the Lord, the source of his strength. He frequently spoke of his help coming from the Lord (Psalm 121:2). This is why Isaiah 40:28-31 assures us that "God gives power to the weak, And to those who have no might He increases strength. But those who wait on the Lord shall renew their strength." While it is God's default position to give power and strength, something happened that introduced a condition for receiving the strength He inherently provides.

Angels, on the other hand, are purely spiritual beings with spiritual bodies, although they have the ability to transform and manifest in physical form.

However, this is not their default state. Angels do not possess a soul in the same sense as humans. They do not share the triune nature of humans. Therefore, when angels sin, they are instantly judged, just like the Devil and his fallen angels. Angels are seen as celestial beings tasked with carrying out divine assignments and do not possess the same characteristics as humans, such as mortality or the need for salvation.

As human beings, due to our composition, we have the ability to receive salvation. As mentioned earlier, we live from the core of our triune nature, either as living souls or dead souls. Hence, we embark on evangelistic endeavours to win souls, not spirits or bodies. We are called soul winners. The Bible also warns about the loss of the soul in Matthew 16:26, "For what is a man profited if he gains the whole world, and loses his own soul? Or what will a man give in exchange for his soul?"

Therefore, when God commanded Adam that on the day he eats, he would surely die (Genesis 2:17), He was referring to the soul, as clarified in Ezekiel 18:4,20, "The soul that sins, it shall die." However, the devil, the master deceiver, misled man into thinking it referred to the death of the body, thus deceiving man into disobeying God.

In the current state of being alive and residing in our human bodies, we are presented with a precious opportunity to receive the gift of salvation through the Holy Spirit. Jesus, before His departure, ensured that the Holy Spirit would remain with us on earth to be our constant companion, as stated in John 14:16. Therefore, while the Holy Spirit continues to work by convicting individuals of their sins, today is the appointed time for salvation. It is crucial not to delay, for tomorrow may be too late, as the moment our spirits depart from our earthly bodies and awaken on the other side, the next event will be to await the day of judgment.

We must not risk facing the same judgment as the devil. Instead, we must repent now and make Jesus the Lord and Saviour of our lives. Allow the abundant life of Christ, the Zoe life, to revive your once-dead soul and enable you to live in righteousness. By doing so, your portion will be secured with God for all of eternity.

***

Can any Good Thing Come Out of the Flesh?
When the spirit is poured out, as prophesied in Joel 2:28, the key qualification to receive it is being flesh, that is, having a human physical body. This is what the text reveals. However, if we were to ask Christians what they believe qualifies them for the things of the Spirit, many would likely respond with "spirituality." It is common for people to strive to develop their spirits, seeking spiritual things. Yet God declares that He will pour out His Spirit based on our fleshly qualification. Being physical is a qualifying factor. This understanding challenges the notion that the flesh is inherently evil and corrupt, as stated by Paul in Romans 7:18 when he said, "For I know that in me (that is, in my flesh) dwelleth no good thing."

However, it is essential to note that the term "flesh" can have different meanings. It can refer to the corrupt system of evil introduced by the devil through the fall of man, known as carnality. On the other hand, it can simply denote the physical state of a human being, encompassing the physical body.

As we begin to recognize the value and advantage of our flesh, viewing it as a qualification, we come to appreciate how our composition as human beings provides us with the opportunity to be saved and to have the Spirit poured out upon us. This privilege is not granted to angels, as they were not created in the likeness of God with a triune body possessing flesh.

The pouring out of God's Spirit is meant for all flesh, as the Spirit is not seeking spirits but flesh. Surprisingly, we tend to believe that being in the flesh disqualifies us from spiritual things. However, there are certain things that can only be obtained in the flesh. Even the greatest gift of salvation cannot be received without being in the flesh. This is evident by the fact that angels, who are spiritual beings and not fleshly beings, never had the opportunity for salvation. Furthermore, when we, as fleshly beings, die and the spirit departs from the body (as mentioned in James 2:26, "For as the body without the spirit is dead"), and we exist as spiritual beings (as indicated by Jesus in Matthew

22:30, "For in the resurrection they neither marry, nor are given in marriage, but are as the angels of God in heaven"), we can no longer be born again if we hadn't already experienced salvation before death, that is when we were still in the human flesh. Therefore, the qualification for salvation is the flesh.

However, prior to your death, preachers and others were instructing you not to focus on the flesh. They portrayed everything about the flesh as wicked and evil, suggesting that there was nothing good about it. This has led many to believe that the flesh disqualifies them from spiritual matters. Yet, without the flesh, you could not even experience being born again. The qualification to undergo a second birth, which is a spiritual birth, is based on the first experience of being born in the flesh. Jesus affirmed this in John 3:5, saying, "Verily, verily, I say unto thee, Except a man (that is flesh) be born of water and of the Spirit, he cannot enter into the kingdom of God. That which is born of the flesh is flesh, and that which is born of the Spirit is spirit. Marvel not that I said unto thee, Ye must be born again." Therefore, to be born again, one must have experienced the first birth, which is of the flesh, in order to be qualified for the second birth, which is spiritual. As stated in 1 Corinthians 15:46, "Howbeit that was not first which is spiritual, but that which is natural; and afterward that which is spiritual."

The first man, Adam, was of the flesh, and we have all experienced the earthly nature through our inheritance. This qualifies us to experience the last Adam, who is spiritual, as stated in 1 Corinthians 15:47, "The first man is of the earth, earthy; the second man is the Lord from heaven. As is the earthy, such are they also that are earthy: and as is the heavenly, such are they also that are heavenly. And as we have borne the image of the earthy, we shall also bear the image of the heavenly."

Through one man, Adam, sin entered the world, and we all inherited sin. But through the obedience of one man, the Lord Jesus, the spiritual life that we lost in the Garden of Eden has become available to make many righteous through faith. Romans 5:19 declares, "For as by one man's disobedience many were made sinners, so by the obedience of one shall many be made righteous."

Although the spiritual life is now available to us, it is crucial to understand the source through which this provision was made. It was not a spirit that died in place of a man's sin. This is why the conversion had to occur. The Word had to become flesh, as stated in John 1:14, "And the Word was made flesh, and dwelt among us." It was the flesh that qualified Jesus to take our place as a substitute and die to pay the penalty of sin, thus making salvation available to all flesh. Titus 2:11 confirms this truth: "For the grace of God that bringeth salvation hath appeared to all men."

Without the flesh, Jesus would not have qualified to die for our sins, as you cannot kill a spirit. If Jesus had come solely as God or a spirit being, they would not have been able to put Him to death. However, Jesus willingly became a human being, taking on 100% flesh, for the purpose of His sacrificial death. Hebrews 2:9 affirms this: "But we see Jesus, who was made a little lower than the angels for the suffering of death." He willingly set aside His divinity and assumed humanity. Philippians 2:7 states, "But made himself of no reputation, and took upon him the form of a servant, and was made in the likeness of men." Jesus needed flesh, a physical human body, in order to accomplish salvation for us. Hebrews 10:5 reveals that a body was prepared for Him: "Wherefore when he cometh into the world, he saith, Sacrifice and offering thou wouldest not, but a body hast thou prepared me."

The flesh is like an indispensable adversary, but one must be cautious to extract the good and avoid the influence of the bad. It is remarkable that the very same flesh, which was weak through carnality and unable to please God in fulfilling the law, is also necessary as a physical human body for the condemnation of sin. As stated in Romans 8:3, "For what the law could not do, in that it was weak through the flesh, God sending his own Son in the likeness of sinful flesh, and for sin, condemned sin in the flesh." This unveils the mystery of the human flesh.

While the flesh can be associated with evil and corruption, there are numerous benefits and privileges we derive from being in the flesh. The key distinction is preventing the flesh from influencing us through the love of its desires, the stimulation of the five senses, or the alternative system of carnality that the devil has created. Instead, we should utilize the flesh, our physical human body, as a tool to advance our spiritual journey while we are still on Earth. It is through the flesh that the spirit is granted a legal right to operate in this world. Therefore, we must learn to yield our physical bodies as vessels that the Holy Spirit can utilize, as mentioned in 1 Corinthians 6:19, "What? Know ye not that your body is the temple of the Holy Ghost which is in you, which ye have of God, and ye are not your own?"

To illustrate the nature of our relationship with the flesh, let us consider our relationship with the world. The world is corrupt, and as emphasized by Jesus in 1 John 2:15, we are instructed not to love the world or its possessions. He states, "Love not the world, neither the things that are in the world. If any man love the world, the love of the Father is not in him." However, in John 17:15, we witness Jesus praying, "I pray not that thou shouldest take them out of the world, but that thou shouldest keep them from the evil." This demonstrates that although we are in the world, we are not of the world.

Similarly, although we are in the flesh, we are not defined by it. We ought to allow the Holy Spirit to have control over our flesh, just as Paul did. We must not conform to the patterns of this world, as stated in Romans 12:2. Likewise, we should not conform to the system of carnality. Instead, we should extract the good from the flesh and utilize it for the advancement of our spirituality.

Furthermore, we can trust that just as Jesus prayed for God to protect us from evil, even while we are in this corrupt flesh, Jesus is capable of keeping us from stumbling and yielding to the desires and carnality of the flesh. He can present us faultless before His presence, as mentioned in Jude 1:24.

Chapter 4

The Flesh, The World and The Devil

The Birth of the Flesh

After Lucifer's unsuccessful attempt to exalt himself above God and be worshipped as God, he settled for a lesser plan. The devil devised a scheme to establish a rival realm to that of God's. He knew precisely how to achieve this. By enticing humans to rebel against God through disobedience, he could bring forth a rival realm known as the Flesh. It is essential to understand that the term "Flesh," birthed by sin, does not refer to the human body that God created from the dust of the earth. Rather, it signifies a system or realm called Carnality. Since the fall of mankind, the terms "Flesh" and "Carnal" have been used interchangeably.

In order to create this alternate system, the devil required human involvement. Being a deceiver, liar, and cunning being, the devil presented a proposition to humanity. His proposition was to make man, who was already created in God's image and likeness, become like God. Genesis 3:5 states, "For God doth know that in the day ye eat thereof, then your eyes shall be opened, and ye shall be as gods, knowing good and evil." It was a strange proposition indeed, as it sought to make someone what they already were. However, through cunningness, the devil managed to sell this inferior rival god system, the Flesh, to humanity, and they fell for it as described in Genesis 3:6, "And when the woman saw that the tree was good for food and that it was pleasant to the eyes and a tree to be desired to make one wise, she took of the fruit thereof and did eat, and gave also unto her husband with her; and he did eat."

By deceiving humanity, the devil achieved at least three benefits for his agenda: The Birth of the Flesh, The world, and The Devil's Agenda. These can be observed in the temptation of Jesus by the devil:

Sin created an alternative realm for the devil to advance his agenda of being worshipped as God. This rival realm, known as the Flesh, stands in complete opposition to God's realm. In Galatians 5:17, it is described as "contrary": "For the flesh lusteth against the Spirit, and the Spirit against the flesh; and these are contrary the one to the other, so that ye cannot do the things that ye would."

We have been created for God's pleasure to worship and have fellowship with Him, but the realm activated by the devil through sin hinders us from fulfilling our purpose, as stated in Ecclesiastes 12:13, "Let us hear the conclusion of the whole matter: Fear God and keep his commandments, for this is the whole duty of man."

Sin gave birth to a realm that leads humanity to do the exact opposite of its duty. Man rebels against God and disobeys His commands. This makes man a slave to sin, obedient to the devil's commands, and effectively worshipping him.

The devil deceived humanity by offering them wisdom, as described in Genesis 3:6, "And when the woman saw that the tree was good for food and that it was pleasant to the eyes and a tree to be desired to make one wise, she took of the fruit thereof and did eat, and gave also unto her husband with her; and he did eat." However, the wisdom they gained was inferior. In 1 Corinthians 3:18–21, it is written, "Let no man deceive himself. If any man among you seems to be wise in this world, let him become a fool so that he may be wise. For the wisdom of this world is foolishness with God. For it is written, He takes the wise in their own craftiness. And again, The Lord knows the thoughts of the wise, that they are vain. Therefore, let no man glory in men. For all things are yours."

The Bible warns in Proverbs 16:25, "There is a way that seemeth right unto a man, but the end thereof are the ways of death."

Before the fall, humans were spiritual beings created in God's likeness but dwelling in bodies made of dust. They were unashamed of their nakedness (Genesis 2:25).

However, when their eyes were opened to the realm of the Flesh, shame emerged, leading them to cover themselves (Genesis 3:7).

With this awakening, they became aware of the Flesh, a separate consciousness and will from God. The system of the Flesh cannot fulfil God's law and is contrary to the Spirit.

Isaiah 55:7-9 emphasizes the contrast between these systems. It calls for the wicked to forsake their ways and thoughts, returning to the Lord, who offers abundant pardon. God's ways and thoughts are higher than those of humans, just as the heavens are higher than the earth.

The Flesh was the first temptation the devil presented to Jesus, as recorded in Luke 4:3-4. "And the devil said unto him, If thou be the Son of God, command this stone that it be made bread. And Jesus answered him, saying, It is written, That man shall not live by bread alone, but by every word of God."

Jesus, after completing his fast and experiencing physical hunger, faced temptation from the devil. The devil took advantage of Jesus' hunger in the flesh, but Jesus overcame it by shifting his focus away from the flesh. If Jesus had considered his physical condition, he might have yielded to the temptation of turning stones into bread. He would have satisfied his immediate physical hunger but potentially jeopardized his sonship, just as Esau traded his birth right for a single meal. However, unlike the first Adam, who accepted a substandard reality, Jesus understood what truly mattered and turned to the Spirit. He recognized that people need the word of God, not just physical food, to truly live.

The birth of the flesh, the emergence of the carnal realm, stands as the primary benefit the devil obtained through the fall of humanity. It became his rival domain, opposing the realm of God and drawing individuals away from a life focused on the Spirit and aligned with His will.

***

The World

It is important to distinguish between the world and the earth. The earth refers to the physical elements and materials, while the world represents a system. Psalm 24:1 states, "The earth is the Lord's, and the fullness thereof; the world, and they that dwell therein." The semicolon in the verse elaborates on the fullness of the earth, including the world (systems) and its inhabitants (people, plants, animals, etc.).

God created everything good, including the world (systems), but sin introduced corruption. Nevertheless, God demonstrated his love for the world by sending his Son as a propitiation to reconcile the world back to himself.

The earth can be likened to money, and the love for money represents the world. Money itself is not inherently evil, but the love for it gives rise to evils such as greed and covetousness. This love for money can drive people to the point of desperation in their pursuit of wealth. As stated in 1 Timothy 6:10, "For the love of money is the root of all evil: which while some coveted after, they have erred from the faith, and pierced themselves through with many sorrows." Similarly, the earth and material possessions are good in themselves, but when the world (systems and things in the world) becomes active, it leads to lust. 1 John 2:15 warns, "Love not the world, neither the things that are in the world. If any man love the world, the love of the Father is not in him." The verse goes on to explain what the things in the world are: "For all that is in the world, the lust of the flesh, and the lust of the eyes, and the pride of life, is not of the Father, but is of the world" (1 John 2:16). It is important to note that the world and its lusts are temporary, but those who do the will of God abide forever.

The systems encompassed by the world also include kingdoms, which represent authority, rule, or power. This was the second way in which the devil benefited from the fall of man. He got the authority & powers of the world from man and installed himself as the god of this world.

During Jesus' second temptation, as described in Luke 4:5, the devil took him to a high mountain and showed him all the kingdoms of the world in an instant.

The devil claimed that he possessed the power and glory of these kingdoms, as stated in verse 6, "And the devil said unto him, All this power will I give thee, and the glory of them, for that is delivered unto me; and to whomsoever I will I give it." The devil referred to the kingdoms as power and glory, which were the keys he had deceitfully taken from Adam, who was originally given dominion over the earth.

The devil, desiring worship, tempted Jesus with a proposition: "If thou therefore wilt worship me, all shall be thine" (Luke 4:7). However, Jesus firmly replied, "Get thee behind me, Satan: for it is written, Thou shalt worship the Lord thy God, and him only shalt thou serve" (Luke 4:8). True worship is exclusively reserved for the one true God, as Jesus taught: "But the hour cometh, and now is, when the true worshippers shall worship the Father in spirit and in truth: for the Father seeketh such to worship him" (John 4:23). Therefore, worshiping in the flesh is directed towards the devil, as it aligns with a rival system that cannot satisfy or please God.

The devil continues to employ this tactic, using the allure of the world to entice individuals into worshiping him. He offers them the entire world in exchange for their souls, as expressed in Matthew 16:26, "For what is a man profited, if he shall gain the whole world, and lose his own soul? or what shall a man give in exchange for his soul?". His ultimate goal is to be worshipped, and he will persist in this ambition until he faces final judgment. In future events during the great tribulation, as described in Revelation 13:4, the devil, also known as the dragon, will seek worship: "And they worshipped the dragon which gave power unto the beast: and they worshipped the beast, saying, Who is like unto the beast? who is able to make war with him?"

Furthermore, anyone who refuses to worship him will face death, as revealed in Revelation 13:15, "And he had power to give life unto the image of the beast, that the image of the beast should both speak, and cause that as many as would not worship the image of the beast should be killed."

Do not be deceived by the enemy's lies. Whatever he offers or dictates to you is merely in support of his agenda to be worshipped. Stand against the devil. Reject his agenda, pursue righteousness, and worship the one true God of heaven by obeying his commands through the life, strength, and grace provided by Jesus Christ.

***

The Devil's Agenda

The devil is exceedingly self-centred, willing to go to any extent to make himself the centre of attention. Just as he brought about death for humanity, he attempted the same strategy with Jesus during the temptation.

By taking Jesus to a high pinnacle, his intention was to deceitfully lure Jesus into jumping, fully aware that Jesus, though divine, was in human flesh at that time and that jumping would result in death. The devil hoped that Jesus would yield to his temptation, allowing the devil to reign freely as the god of the world without any rival or hope of salvation for his subjects. It is important to remember that the devil's agenda to remove God from the world began in the Garden of Eden, and his efforts to eliminate Jesus started even before His birth, as seen in Herod's massacre of the male infants in an attempt to find and destroy Jesus.

In Luke 4:9, it is written: "And he brought him to Jerusalem, and set him on a pinnacle of the temple, and said unto him, If thou be the Son of God, cast thyself down from hence: For it is written, He shall give his angels charge over thee, to keep thee; And in their hands they shall bear thee up, lest at any time thou dash thy foot against a stone." Jesus responded in verse 12, saying, "It is said, Thou shalt not tempt the Lord thy God." Jesus emphasized through the Word that the Lord God should not be tempted. He did not succumb to the temptation of calling upon angels to rescue Him or performing a spiritual feat as the Son of God to prove to the devil that He was capable of such acts.

This devil, being the central figure in the entire scheme, had the ultimate desire to be God. This was the final benefit the devil derived from the fall of humanity. Through the introduction of death, he became the Father. "Father" implies being a source, and while we know that God is the source of life, when the devil caused humanity to sin, he became the source of death, lies, and evil.

John 8:44 states, "Ye are of your father the devil, and the lusts of your father ye will do. He was a murderer from the beginning and abode not in the truth, because there is no truth in him. When he speaks a lie, he speaks of his own; for he is a liar and the father of it."

Anyone who rejects Christ is, by default, a slave to sin. In other words, they have the devil as their source (the Father). Consequently, their lives, behaviour, actions, decisions, and so forth offer the worship that the devil desperately craves. Do not have the devil as your Father. Through the Lord Jesus, you can be reconciled to your heavenly Father.

Chapter 5

The Fall and Death of the Living Soul

The Fall of Man and the Consequences of Sin

It was God's divine responsibility to sustain, commune, communicate, and bestow life upon man, who was created in His image and likeness. Therefore, He would visit man in the cool of the day, speaking to the spirit within him, and the soul accurately conveyed this message to Adam's human body. In perfect harmony, Adam's body responded to God through his soul. This harmonious relationship restored peace, unity, and tranquillity between heaven and earth following the fall of Lucifer and his angels.

However, when God created man, He gave a clear command with dire consequences if disobeyed. This instruction and its consequences are found in Genesis 2:17, "But of the tree of the knowledge of good and evil you shall not eat, for in the day that you eat of it you shall surely die."

God, in His wisdom, gave specific instructions to safeguard humanity from the power of death. Before the creation of mankind, the devil had already committed sin, bringing death into the world. The devil's arrogance and desire to be equal to God resulted in sin, and when sin matured, it brought forth death (James 1:15). To counter the devastating effects of death, God provided the tree of life for humanity to partake of. However, access to this tree would be restricted if humans disobeyed God's command, ultimately leading to the certainty of death.

God's instruction to Adam was not a temptation but a means to preserve him from the activation of death, which was brought into existence by the devil's prior sin. The devil's prideful desire to be like God conceived sin, and sin, when fully grown, gave birth to death (James 1:15). Therefore, the purpose of the instruction was to prevent man from introducing death into his world, just as the devil had done before him.

To demonstrate that God did not place the tree of the knowledge of good and evil in the Garden of Eden to tempt man, we find evidence in the fact that God had already established a redemption plan from the foundation of the world. Revelation 13:8 speaks of "the Lamb slain from the foundation of the world." This plan of redemption existed alongside the instruction, affirming God's intention to provide a way for restoration if man were to fall.

But why would God establish a redemption plan if He truly did not want man to fall? It can be likened to someone purchasing insurance for a new automobile before even driving it out of the showroom. One might wonder if the insurance was obtained because the person intended to crash the car immediately. Certainly not. The reason behind acquiring insurance is the awareness that one will be driving on roads filled with inexperienced and dangerous drivers. Therefore, having insurance serves as a safeguard in case something adverse happens, ensuring there is a plan for replacing or restoring the damaged automobile to its original state.

Likewise, death was already conceived through the fall of Lucifer and his angels, and God's purpose was to prevent man from experiencing the same fate. God did not create man with the intention of causing his downfall; death was not part of the equation when man was initially formed. However, God was fully aware that the devil and his fallen angels, like inexperienced and dangerous drivers, were active and prone to luring men into temptation and disobedience.

In anticipation of such an event, God established the insurance plan of redemption.

The Scriptures affirm that God does not tempt anyone, as stated in James 1:13: "Let no one say when he is tempted, 'I am tempted by God, for God cannot be tempted by evil, nor does He Himself tempt anyone." Therefore, God's intention was not to tempt man but to provide a means of escape and redemption in the face of temptation. God's desire, even after the fall of man and the activation of the redemption plan through His Son Jesus Christ, is revealed in 2 Peter 3:9, where it is stated that He is "not willing that any should perish, but that all should come to repentance." It is clear that God did not lure men into sinning against Him only to desire their repentance later.

The devil, known for his deceitfulness and cunning nature (Genesis 3:1), understood the workings of temptation well. Having successfully deceived and led one-third of the angels to rebel against God, he used this knowledge to approach Eve and bring about the perfect conditions for her to succumb to his temptation.

Temptation preys on desire or lust. The devil couldn't force Eve to eat from the forbidden tree, but he could sow a desire within her by selling her a lie. By believing the lie, desire was birthed. The devil, desiring to establish an alternate system to God's, needed mankind on his side. However, in order to cause them to rebel and disobey God, he had to come up with a cunning idea that would entice them. He presented them with the false notion of becoming like God, insinuating that God was hiding the ability to discern good and evil from them. He painted a picture of a new wisdom that would be unveiled through the opening of their conscious eyes. Genesis 3:6 tells us, "And when the woman saw that the tree was good for food and that it was pleasant to the eyes and a tree to be desired to make one wise, she took of the fruit thereof and did eat, and gave also unto her husband with her; and he did eat." The devil's temptation was perfected when he successfully convinced the woman of the goodness of the tree and what she was missing out on. This birthed a desire within her, compelling her to reach out and take the fruit with her own hands, disobeying God and succumbing to the devil's temptation, thus sinning against God.

When we yield to temptation, it is often because of the lust or desire within us that we seek to satisfy. However, yielding to temptation gives birth to sin. And sin, when fully grown, brings forth death. Therefore, when man sinned, death was introduced into the world (James 1:15).

***

The Triune Nature of Man and the Effects of Death

It is crucial to understand that the soul, when in a state of spiritual death, is unable to interpret or receive spiritual communication. Instead, it can only engage in fleshly, carnal communication through the five senses, driven by the lust of the flesh, the lust of the eyes, and the pride of life. However, Romans 8:13 states, "For if ye live after the flesh, ye shall die." Therefore, death is the inevitable outcome for a soul that is sourced or fuelled by the flesh.

Death is a state of separation. James 2:26 affirms, "For as the body without the spirit is dead." When God initially created man, it was His spirit that infused life into the soul, and the soul, in turn, animated the physical body. However, after Adam sinned, he fell short of the glory of God. As a consequence, God's spirit departed from man, and the devil seized the opportunity to manipulate the soul through the influence of the five senses. This allowed the devil to establish an alternative system to that of God. While God is spirit, the devil became the master of the flesh realm. Hence, the flesh was created as an alternative system to God, resulting in a conflict between the flesh and the spirit. As stated in the Scripture, the flesh lusts against the spirit, and they are contrary to one another.

To illustrate this concept, we can liken the flesh to a smart mobile phone without a SIM card. The phone itself possesses various capabilities and functions, but without a connection to a cellular tower for interconnection with the web and other networks, it falls short of its full potential. In this disconnected state, the phone can still perform local functions but cannot receive or send signals. It remains limited and unable to access the full range of its intended capabilities.

Similarly, when man is separated from the Spirit of God, his flesh operates in a restricted manner, disconnected from the spiritual realm. Though he may engage in worldly activities, his soul is unable to establish a true connection with God and receive the spiritual signals and guidance intended for him. This disconnection hinders man from reaching his full potential and experiencing the abundant life that comes from being aligned with God's purposes.

It is important to recognize that there is a way that may appear right or attractive to man in his fleshly state, but without the spiritual connection and guidance of God, it ultimately leads to spiritual emptiness and unfulfillment. Only by reconnecting with the Spirit of God and aligning ourselves with His will can we truly experience an abundant life and fulfill our intended purpose.

When the source of life is severed, those dependent on it are destined to die. Jesus Himself stated in John 15:6, "If a man abides not in me, he is cast forth as a branch and is withered." Withering is a gradual process. A branch that is disconnected from the tree may initially appear green and vibrant, but over time, it begins to dry up, showing signs of lifelessness until it eventually withers away. Similarly, the process of death in humanity starts with the spirit and gradually affects the other aspects of our triune being.

Man, as a triune being, experienced death at three different stages of his existence. The first stage was the death of the spirit. When Man sinned, God withdrew His presence from him, resulting in the separation of God's spirit from man's spirit. This separation led to the immediate death of the spirit. The spirit of man relies on the Spirit of God as the source of life for the soul, and the soul, in turn, sustains the body. Therefore, if one were to destroy the body and soul, the most effective place to start would be at the source.

When God created the fish, He spoke to the sea; when He created the trees, He spoke to the earth. However, when He created man, He spoke to Himself. God spoke directly to the source of each of His creatures. So, how does one kill a creature? Simply by separating it from its source. This is why a fish dies when taken out of the sea, a tree dies when uprooted from the earth, and when man is separated from his source—the Spirit of Life (Ruach)—he dies. The consequence of this separation was the death of the spirit in man. James 4:5

says, "Do ye think that the scripture saith in vain, The spirit that dwelleth in us lusteth to envy?" This is not the Spirit of God that gives life, but the resulting spirit of man after the fall.

Events in the spiritual realm occur almost instantaneously, and their physical manifestations unfold over time. This is why the devil was immediately judged and has no chance of forgiveness, as he sinned in his state as a spirit being. On the other hand, man, being a triune being, has the opportunity for forgiveness while still in his human body. However, once he transitions into a spirit being through physical death, judgment follows. The death of the spirit marked the beginning of the death process for the other components of man's triune being.

The death of the soul was activated by the instantaneous death of the spirit, but the death of the soul occurred gradually. While man's soul was dying, he could still communicate with God, just as Cain, in his sinful state, negotiated with God. However, Scripture tells us that once Cain concluded the dialogue, he went out of the presence of the Lord (Genesis 4:13–16).

The devil's primary focus was the soul, as it is the core of man's being. If the devil can gain control of the soul, he can gain control of the entire man and manipulate him to rebel against God and worship the devil as God.

With God's Spirit no longer giving life to the soul, the devil seized the opportunity to infuse death into the soul through the works of the flesh. Thus training the soul to default to the flesh for sustenance and, in turn, influencing the Spirit of man to lust.

The final component of man's triune being to experience death is the body. As stated in Genesis 2:17, "In the day that thou eatest thereof, thou shalt surely die." It is important to understand that a day in God's sight is like a thousand years (2 Peter 3:8). Therefore, man's body, which was not initially designed to die, began to experience physical death that day. No man has ever lived up to or beyond a thousand years. The oldest man recorded in the Scriptures, Methuselah, lived for 969 years before his death. For those individuals whom God desired to spare from death, He took them out of the earth, such as Enoch and Elijah.

Chapter 6

The Corrupted Soul and God's Displeasure

The Corruption of the Soul and the Alternate System

When God created man, He communicated with him through His Spirit dwelling within him. In those moments, God would visit man in the cool of the day. However, when man fell and God's Spirit departed, a new system emerged—the flesh, characterized by carnality. It is essential to recognize that man possesses free will, which he can exercise without God's interference. As the death of man's soul reached completion, the natural line of communication between man and God ceased. It was only when man realized his inability to hear God that he exercised his free will to invite God back into earthly affairs. This birthed a new mode of communication known as prayer, as stated in Genesis 4:26, "Then began men to call upon the name of the Lord."

Prayer, a system established by God, serves as an invitation to bring Him into the world, restoring the lost channel of communication. Through prayer, we grant God permission to operate in the earth, creating an open portal for Him to fulfill His purposes through our yielded vessels. Although Satan believed his alternate system was perfected upon the completion of the death of the soul, his assumption proved to be incorrect.

Seeking to corrupt the already dead soul, Satan employed his fallen angels to take on physical forms and marry the daughters of men. This diabolical plan sealed the deal, perfecting the alternate system. Consequently, the outcome was a soul capable of only one thing: evil. Genesis 6:5 reveals the depth of man's wickedness, stating, "And God saw that the wickedness of man was great in the earth, and that every imagination of the thoughts of his heart was only evil continually." Through the corruption of the soul, the adversary aimed to ensure that man's thoughts and intentions were constantly inclined towards evil.

Genesis 6:11–12 further states, "The earth also was corrupt before God, and the earth was filled with violence. And God looked upon the earth, and, behold, it was corrupt; for all flesh had corrupted his way upon the earth."

This corruption severed ties with God, replacing the source that once fed the soul with the stimuli of the flesh's five senses rather than the Spirit of life from God. When the Spirit was disconnected and died, the soul needed a new source of nourishment. The devil took advantage of the five senses, influencing the soul through the lust of the eyes, the lust of the flesh, and the pride of life. Man's soul was now predisposed to continuous evil, corrupting the spirit in the process. The Bible addresses the dead spirit of man in James 4:5, "Do you think that the Scripture says in vain, 'The spirit that dwells in us lusts to envy?'" This refers not to the Spirit of life (ruach) that departed from man but rather to the corrupted spirit of man.

The realm of prayer is deeply spiritual, and the devil's aim is to establish a parallel system that excludes God. In his quest, he introduces corruption to an already dead soul. This corruption leads to a state where the intent of man's heart becomes solely and continuously evil, thus fulfilling the devil's objective of pushing God out and creating an alternate system that stands in opposition.

It is evident that the devil comprehends the concept of corruption, as depicted in Matthew 12:33: "Either make the tree good and his fruit good; or else make the tree corrupt and his fruit corrupt; for the tree is known by his fruit." The devil knows which strings to pull. By successfully corrupting the soul of man, the desire to call upon God or seek Him in any way is extinguished. This aligns with Matthew 7:17, which states, "Every good tree bringeth forth good fruit; but a corrupt tree bringeth forth evil fruit." Verse 18 emphasizes the hopelessness of expecting anything good from something that is corrupt: "A good tree cannot bring forth evil fruit, nor can a corrupt tree bring forth good fruit."

***

The Alternate System's exclusion of God and the Hopelessness of Corruption

The corruption of all flesh was so severe that no one sought God through prayer. The devil, in his pursuit of perfecting the fall of man, established an alternate system devoid of any knowledge of God through corruption.

As Psalm 14:1 states, "The fool hath said in his heart, There is no God. They are corrupt; they have done abominable works; there is none that doeth good." The Lord, looking down from heaven upon the children of men, found that there were none who understood or sought after God. All had gone astray and become defiled; not a single person was found to be righteous or good.

In this corrupt state, the flesh became incapable of engaging in anything spiritual. The natural man, as stated in 1 Corinthians 2:14, does not receive the things of the Spirit of God. To him, they are foolishness, and he cannot understand them because they are spiritually discerned. The soul of man, once able to call upon God even in its dead state, has now lost that ability due to corruption. Prayer, which was once a voluntary system for inviting God to rule in one's affairs, became an impossible task for the flesh, for the devil never desired God's presence to begin with.

For anyone seeking to approach God in prayer, spiritual enablement is necessary, as highlighted in Psalm 80:18. The plea is made, "So will not we go back from thee; quicken us, and we will call upon thy name." The term "quicken" means to give life. Thus, the flesh now requires the life of the spirit for the willingness and desire to pray to be birthed. In this state of corruption, prayer becomes more than a mere human endeavour; it becomes a divine intervention where God imparts His life and enables us to commune with Him.

In the garden of Gethsemane, we witness Jesus instructing His disciples, saying, "Sit ye here while I go and pray yonder." He then takes Peter and the two sons of Zebedee with Him and begins to be sorrowful and heavy. Jesus says to them, "My soul is exceeding sorrowful, even unto death; tarry ye here and watch with me." In this context, to "watch" means to be vigilant and engaged in prayer.

However, upon returning from His time of prayer, Jesus finds His disciples asleep, as stated in Matthew 26:40, "And he cometh unto the disciples, and findeth them asleep, and saith unto Peter, What, could ye not watch with me one hour?" During this period, the Holy Spirit had not yet been given, and the disciples were still predominantly operating in the flesh rather than relying on the aid of the Spirit. Jesus emphasizes a crucial factor that assists a person in their fleshly state to facilitate prayer. In verse 41, He declares, "Watch and pray, that ye enter not into temptation: the spirit indeed is willing, but the flesh is weak."

Jesus's words provide valuable insight into the relationship between watching, praying, and overcoming temptation. He urges His disciples, and by extension, us, to be vigilant and watchful in prayer, recognizing the inherent weakness of the flesh. While the spirit may be willing, the flesh tends to be weak and susceptible to yielding to temptation. Therefore, Jesus encourages us to remain watchful and prayerful to avoid falling into temptation.

This passage not only portrays the struggle Jesus faced in His humanity but also reveals the importance of being alert in prayer. It reminds us that, even in our fleshly state, we can find strength and victory through watchful prayer. By relying on the aid of the Holy Spirit and maintaining a vigilant posture in prayer, we can overcome the weaknesses of the flesh and resist the temptations that seek to hinder our walk with God.

Engaging in prayer, which is a spiritual form of communication, poses a significant challenge for mankind without the presence of the Holy Spirit. Paul emphasizes this truth in Romans 8:26: "Likewise the Spirit also helpeth our infirmities; for we know not what we should pray for as we ought, but the Spirit itself maketh intercession for us with groanings that cannot be uttered." This highlights the vital role of the Holy Spirit in our prayer lives.

Understanding the limitations of the flesh, Jesus, after His death, chose to send us the Holy Spirit. He recognized that, as stated in Luke 18:1, "men ought always to pray and not to faint." However, He also knew that individuals in their fleshly state had little chance of fulfilling this spiritual activity. Without a means of communication that invites God to rule in the affairs of humanity, the establishment of God's kingdom on earth becomes impossible.

When Jesus taught us to pray, one of the fundamental aspects He highlighted was the coming of God's kingdom and the fulfillment of His will on earth, mirroring its manifestation in heaven. This grand objective can only be accomplished through prayer. It is through prayer that we open a channel for God's reign and divine purposes to be realized in our lives and in the world around us.

Therefore, we recognize the indispensable role of the Holy Spirit in prayer. The Spirit helps us overcome our weaknesses and guides us in our petitions, interceding on our behalf with unutterable groans. Through the Holy Spirit's presence, we gain access to a deeper level of communion with God, enabling us to align our prayers with His perfect will and usher in His kingdom on earth. Prayer is not a mere human endeavour but a supernatural engagement empowered by the Holy Spirit. It is through prayer that we invite God to intervene in our lives, fulfilling His purposes and establishing His kingdom on earth. Let us, therefore, rely on the Holy Spirit's guidance and assistance as we engage in this spiritual discipline, knowing that He enables us to communicate with God in ways that surpass our natural limitations.

***

The Repentance of God and his Mercy

Following the devastating flood, God's heart was moved, and He made a decision within Himself to prevent the repeated destruction of the world. His boundless mercy led Him to vow never again to bring a flood to destroy all flesh. Genesis 6:11 states, "And I will establish my covenant with you; neither shall all flesh be cut off any more by the waters of a flood; neither shall there any more be a flood to destroy the earth." In this act of repentance, God showed His desire for reconciliation and restoration.

To symbolize this covenant, God set a rainbow in the clouds as a perpetual reminder of His promise. Genesis 9:13–16 declares, "I do set my bow in the cloud, and it shall be for a token of a covenant between me and the earth. And it shall come to pass, when I bring a cloud over the earth, that the bow shall be seen in the cloud. And I will remember my covenant, which is between me and you and every living creature of all flesh; and the waters shall no more become a flood to destroy all flesh. And the bow shall be in the cloud, and I will look upon it, that I may remember the everlasting covenant between God and every living creature of all flesh that is upon the earth."

Through the rainbow, God assures us that His mercy and grace prevail over judgment. It serves as a visible sign of His faithfulness and commitment to never again destroy the earth by flood. Whenever we see the rainbow, we are reminded of God's repentance, His covenant, and His enduring love for all living creatures.

However, subsequent judgments, such as the destruction of Sodom, serve as a powerful reminder of the wrath of God that awaits those who commit evil and reject the offer of salvation through His Son, Jesus Christ. The fire that consumed Sodom represents the impending judgment that will be unleashed upon the ungodly. It is a solemn warning of the consequences of sin and the urgency to repent and turn to Christ for abundant life.

Do not become a victim of the imminent danger that awaits the unrepentant. Embrace the opportunity for salvation that Christ offers, for there is no better time than now. Today is the day of salvation, and we implore you to heed this warning. As the Scriptures declare in 2 Corinthians 5:11, "Knowing therefore the terror of the Lord, we persuade men."

Let your awareness of God's righteous judgment motivate you to make the necessary changes in your life. Repentance and acceptance of Jesus Christ as your Lord and Saviour will secure your eternal well-being and shield you from the impending wrath. God's offer of salvation is extended to all, and His desire is for every person to experience His abundant life.

The message is clear: the judgment of God awaits those who persist in evil and reject the salvation offered through Jesus Christ. The call to repentance is urgent as we recognize the gravity of the Lord's terror. Embrace salvation, heed the warning, and enter into the abundant life that Christ provides. May this appeal stir your heart and lead you to the path of righteousness and eternal safety.

The fleshly nature of man makes it imperative for God's Spirit to not continually strive with him. Thus, there comes a point where God's patience and tolerance towards human sinfulness reach a limit. The corruption of humanity, which fulfilled the devil's desires, was executed flawlessly. It had such a profound impact that it caused God to feel remorse for creating mankind, ultimately leading to a limitation on the human lifespan. As stated in Genesis 6:3, "And the Lord said, My spirit shall not always strive with man, for that he also is flesh; yet his days shall be one hundred and twenty years."

The corruption of the flesh had dire consequences, leading to the introduction of death for the human body. Initially, man was not created with the intention of experiencing death. However, through the fall, death entered the world, as stated in Genesis 2:17, which warns that "in the day that thou eatest thereof, thou shalt surely die." It is worth noting that a day is like a thousand years in the sight of God. So the length of man's existence was reduced to one day.

Yet, after the corruption, the span of human life was drastically diminished to a mere 120 years. This reduction in lifespan affected all of humanity, as all individuals inherited this fallen state. As the Scripture declares, "all have sinned and fallen short of the glory of God."

Corruption played a significant role in the fall of man, leading to the establishment of a rival system that opposed God's authority. The influence of the devil prompted humanity to commit the same sins of pride, rebellion, and the creation of an alternate system, mirroring the devil's own disobedience. As a result, the punishment that was initially unleashed upon the devil and his fallen angels through the flood was now repeated and unleashed upon mankind.

The involvement of angels in the corruption of mankind has resulted in some angels being held in bondage. As 2 Peter 2:4 states, "For if God did not spare angels when they sinned, but cast them into hell and committed them to chains of gloomy darkness to be kept until the judgment," This indicates that these angels have been cast into hell and are confined by chains of darkness until the time of judgment.

Revelation 9:14 further reveals the existence of bound angels, stating, "Saying to the sixth angel, which had the trumpet, 'Loose the four angels, which are bound in the great river Euphrates, And the four angels were loosed, which were prepared for an hour, a day, a month, and a year, to slay the third part of men."

These bound angels are depicted as being restricted in their activities and under the control of divine authority. While they possess the power to influence and cause havoc, their potential is currently being restrained to prevent further harm to mankind. However, a specific time has been appointed for their release, which will occur during the pouring out of God's wrath in the great tribulation. At that appointed time, these angels will be unleashed to execute judgment by slaying a third of men.

Satan, being a cunning deceiver, often works through others to accomplish his evil purposes. Therefore, it is possible that the angels directly responsible for corrupting mankind are the ones who are currently bound, while others, including the devil himself, are still free to roam. The devil, despite being the mastermind behind the corruption, is allowed to move about freely.

***

Out of Course: Man's misalignment from God

The corruption of mankind resulted in a profound misalignment that separated man from God's original design. As Psalm 82:5 states, "They know not, nor will they understand; they walk on in darkness; all the foundations of the earth are out of course." This misalignment has rendered man incapable of connecting with God or desiring fellowship with his Creator. Man, who was meant to reflect God's image and likeness, has fallen so low that he has become mere flesh, subject to suffering the same consequences as the fallen angels or the princes of darkness.

Psalm 82:6 reveals God's original intention for mankind, declaring, "I have said, Ye are gods, and all of you are children of the Most High." However, due to corruption and disobedience, the consequences of death and a fall from grace have befallen humanity, just as they have affected the fallen angels or princes.

The misalignment of man after the fall can be illustrated through a comparison. We can liken the flesh to a smart mobile phone without a SIM card. The phone itself possesses various capabilities and functions, but without a connection to a cellular tower for interconnection with the web and other networks, it falls short of its full potential. In this disconnected state, the phone can still perform local functions but cannot receive or send signals. It remains limited and unable to access the full range of its intended capabilities.

Likewise, when man is separated from the Spirit of God, his flesh operates in a restricted manner, disconnected from the spiritual realm. Though he may engage in worldly activities, his soul is unable to establish a true connection with God and receive the spiritual signals and guidance intended for him. This disconnection hinders man from reaching his full potential and experiencing the abundant life that comes from being aligned with God's purposes.

The Scriptures warn us that there is a way that may seem right or attractive to man in his fleshly state, but without the spiritual connection and guidance of God, it ultimately leads to spiritual emptiness and unfulfillment. Proverbs 14:12 states, "There is a way that seems right to a man, but its end is the way to death." Only by reconnecting with the Spirit of God and aligning ourselves with His will can we truly experience an abundant life and fulfill our intended purpose.

Let us heed this message and seek to establish a deep and intimate connection with God through His Spirit. May we recognize the limitations of our fleshly nature and strive to align ourselves with God's purposes and plans. In doing so, we will unlock our true potential, experience spiritual fulfillment, and walk in the abundant life that God has designed for us.

Chapter 7

The Law as a Schoolmaster

The Introduction of the Law to Reveal the Need for Salvation

After the fall of man, humanity became corrupted and deviated from God's original design. As a result, humans were carnal beings, unable to perform spiritual acts or please God. This sinful and carnal nature was passed down from one generation to another through birth, as stated in Romans 5:14, which tells us that "death reigned from Adam to Moses, even over them that had not sinned after the similitude of Adam's transgression."

It is possible that some individuals during that time might have argued, saying, "I have not sinned by breaking a specific command, like Adam did. The only reason I am condemned to death is because I was born into this world." However, Romans 3:23 makes it clear that "all have sinned and come short of the glory of God."

What they failed to grasp is that even though they had not outwardly manifested the works of the flesh, they had inherited a carnal nature from birth. This nature could only result in one thing: sin. Thus, it was practically impossible for anyone to please God, and they were inherently unrighteous. Just because a time bomb has not detonated does not make it any less dangerous or not a bomb at all. Similarly, the inherited nature of sin makes everyone a sinner by default.

Romans 3:10-18 further reveals the effects of this corruption, portraying hearts that do not seek God, a lack of righteousness, and a lack of understanding of God. All had strayed from the right path, experiencing a profound misalignment with God's intended purpose.

If man were to attempt to please God, the inevitable outcome would be death, as stated in Proverbs 16:25, which says, "There is a way that seemeth right unto a man, but the end thereof are the ways of death."

Despite this truth, men remained obstinate, considering it unjust and unfair because they did not commit the same sin as Adam. They believed that, given the opportunity, they could prove God wrong and show that they were not sinners.

To settle this debate, God chose to demonstrate to man that, in their fallen and corrupted state, they were incapable of producing anything good or pleasing to God. Therefore, God gave them the law to fulfill while still in their fallen, carnal state.

The law itself is spiritual, but man is carnal, as Romans 7:14 states, "For we know that the law is spiritual, but I am carnal, sold under sin." Remember that the flesh, representing carnality, lusts against the Spirit, and they are contrary to one another. Thus, there was no possible way for a natural and carnal man to receive or fulfill a spiritual law. It was an impossible task.

In order to silence all arguments, God introduced the law as a teacher or guardian, knowing full well that no flesh (carnal man) can be justified by the works of the law. Instead, through the law, the knowledge of sin is revealed, as stated in Romans 3:19-20. This revelation causes everyone to recognize their own inadequacy and the need for a savior.

Romans 7:7-8 says, "What shall we say, then? Is the law sinful? Certainly not! Nevertheless, I would not have known what sin was had it not been for the law. For I would not have known what coveting really was if the law had not said, 'You shall not covet.' But sin, seizing the opportunity afforded by the commandment, produced in me every kind of coveting." This verse emphasizes that the law brings awareness of sin. Without the law, people would not have understood the true nature of sin and its impact on their lives.

It is important to recognize that the law cannot justify or make someone righteous. Its purpose is to reveal the sinful nature of humanity and point to the need for faith in Jesus Christ as the means of justification and salvation.

***

The Inadequacy of Human Efforts and Self-Righteousness

In our journey of faith, it is crucial to recognize the inadequacy of human efforts and the dangers of self-righteousness. Although there may not be a specific scripture where a person directly tells God that they can please Him in their own strength, the Bible contains passages that shed light on this topic and caution against overestimating our abilities.

Proverbs 16:2 reminds us that while a person may consider their ways to be pure, it is the Lord who weighs the motives of the heart. We are prone to believe that our actions and intentions are righteous and pleasing to God. However, true righteousness is determined by Him, and He sees beyond our outward appearance to the depths of our hearts.

Proverbs 16:25 further emphasizes the tendency of humans to follow a path that seems right to them but ultimately leads to death. This verse serves as a warning, highlighting the inherent flaw in relying solely on our own understanding and self-perceived righteousness. It reminds us that God's perspective is far greater than our own, and His ways are the path to life.

In Romans 10:2-3, the Apostle Paul addresses his fellow Israelites, who sought to establish their own righteousness before God through religious zeal and observance of the law. However, Paul points out that true righteousness comes from God and is received through faith, not through human effort. Our zeal for God must be based on knowledge and a humble submission to His righteousness, rather than an attempt to earn it through our works.

Galatians 2:16 reinforces the truth that no one can be justified by the works of the law. It is through faith in Jesus Christ that we are justified, not by our own deeds or adherence to the law. This verse emphasizes the futility of relying on our own efforts for justification and underlines the necessity of faith in Christ as the means of salvation.

Similarly, Galatians 3:11 makes it evident that no one can be justified before God by the law. The righteous, as the verse states, live by faith. Faith, not the works of the law, becomes the foundation for our relationship with God and our standing as righteousness before Him.

These verses serve as cautionary reminders against self-righteousness and the belief that we can please God solely through our own strength or efforts. They redirect our focus towards God's righteousness, grace, and the indispensable role of faith. We are called to submit ourselves to His ways, acknowledging that our righteousness is found in Him alone. Let us humbly rely on His grace and seek to live by faith, recognizing our need for His transformative power in our lives.

***

The Law was a Schoolmaster Pointing Us to Christ

The concept of the law being a schoolmaster is a powerful metaphor that reveals the purpose and role of the Mosaic law given to the Israelites in the Old Testament. The New Testament provides insights into this profound truth, guiding us to understand the significance of the law in pointing us to Christ.

Galatians 3:24–25 portrays the law as a tutor, guiding and instructing us until we reach Christ. The law served as a necessary guide, revealing our need for salvation through faith. Its purpose was to lead us to Christ, where we find justification by faith. However, once faith in Christ is established, we are no longer under the tutorship of the law. It becomes the gateway that directs us to the ultimate source of righteousness.

Romans 10:4 further illuminates the relationship between Christ and the law. Christ is the culmination and fulfillment of the law. The law's intricate guidelines and requirements find their ultimate meaning and purpose in Him. Through faith in Christ, righteousness becomes attainable for everyone who believes. The law, in its entirety, was a precursor, pointing us to the One who would bring righteousness to all who trust in Him.

Galatians 3:19 sheds light on the temporal nature of the law. It was added because of human transgressions, acting as a temporary measure until the promised offspring, Jesus Christ, came. The law served as a guide and teacher, imparting understanding and knowledge and preparing hearts for the fulfillment of the promise. Its purpose was to pave the way for the Messiah, who would bring salvation and grace.

Romans 3:20 underlines a critical aspect of the law. It clarifies that righteousness cannot be attained through the works of the law alone. No one can be declared righteous in the sight of God by merely following the law's regulations. Instead, the law serves a vital function in our journey towards righteousness. It makes us conscious of our sins, revealing our desperate need for a saviour. It shows us the impossibility of achieving righteousness through our own efforts, leading us to the recognition that we must rely on Christ alone.

In summary, the law acted as a schoolmaster, guiding and instructing the Israelites and all of humanity. It pointed to the need for salvation through faith in Christ, who fulfills the law and grants righteousness to all who believe. The law was a temporary measure, preparing hearts for the promised Messiah. It brings awareness of sin, humbling us and leading us to embrace the grace and salvation found in Jesus Christ. Let us, therefore, appreciate the profound role of the law as a schoolmaster, directing us to the ultimate source of righteousness and eternal life.

***

The Law Pointing Towards Christ as the Ultimate Solution

The law introduced by Moses points us towards Christ as the ultimate solution to our spiritual predicament. In 2 Corinthians 3:7-8, we learn of the stark contrast between the ministry of death associated with the law and the ministry of the Spirit ushered in by the Lord Jesus. The glory of the ministry of the Spirit far outweighs the glory of the former.

Romans 7:1-6 provides a profound explanation of how Christ has come to redeem us from the dominion of the law. The analogy of a woman bound by the law of her husband helps us grasp the transformative power of our union with Christ. Just as a woman is released from her marital obligations upon the death of her husband, we are set free from the grip of the law through the body of Christ. We are no longer bound by its demands but are now able to be united with Him, producing fruit for God through the newness of the Spirit.

To further clarify this truth, let us delve into an illustrative story:

Imagine a woman married to a demanding husband, Husband Number 1. He has valid expectations, such as cleanliness during menstruation, and provides clear guidelines, like using sanitary pads. However, the woman finds herself incapable of meeting these expectations due to her inherent immaturity caused by her parents' disobedience to the emperor by eating a forbidden fruit they were warned not to eat before she was born. This disobedience caused a change in her parents' DNA structure, leading to her being born immature, which in effect altered her DNA structure and rendered her immature from birth.

Feeling overwhelmed and burdened by her inability to fulfil Husband Number 1's demands, the woman longs for liberation. In her quest, she discovers Husband Number 2, who offers an extraordinary solution to her predicament. Husband Number 2 comprehends the root cause of her immaturity and willingly pays the penalty for her parents' disobedience. He also has a special potion that can cure the woman's present condition.

Husband Number 2 extends a remarkable proposition. He offers her a new life—a life of maturity and capability—exclusively through a marriage union with Him. In this new life, the woman can effortlessly meet the demands Husband Number 1 places upon her, such as changing her sanitary pads, without feeling overwhelmed or burdened. Husband Number 2 fulfils these demands on her behalf but through her. For this to work, he simply asks her to remain connected to Him, prioritising their relationship and relying on Him for the strength to live out the maturity and ability He provides through the potion he supplies.

However, there's a catch. The woman cannot marry Husband Number 2 while Husband Number 1 is alive, as divorce is not an option. The only way to nullify her marriage with Husband Number 1 is through his death. Yet, Husband Number 1 enjoys good health and is expected to live to an old age. Breaking free from the demands of Husband Number 1 appears impossible without resorting to extreme measures.

But here comes the astonishing twist. Husband Number 2 possesses supernatural abilities to give life and resurrect the woman from her state of immaturity. He can raise her from the dead. The choice now rests with the woman. She must decide whether she is willing to die to her old self, her immaturity, and the demands of Husband Number 1. Through this courageous decision, she can be united in marriage with Husband Number 2 and enjoy the new conditions and fulfilment He offers.

This powerful illustration beautifully represents Husband Number 1 as the justified demands of the law, which the woman, due to her immaturity, cannot fulfil. Husband Number 2 symbolises Jesus Christ, who pays the penalty for her parents' disobedience and grants her a new life of maturity and capability. Through her union with Husband Number 2, the woman receives the necessary resources to fulfil the demands that were once unattainable for her.

This concept aligns wonderfully with the truth conveyed in Galatians 2:20: "I have been crucified with Christ. It is no longer I who live, but Christ who lives in me. And the life I now live in the flesh, I live by faith in the Son of God, who loved me and gave Himself for me." Through our union with Christ, a profound transformation occurs. Our immaturity is replaced by maturity, and we can fulfil the demands of the law through the life and ability He supplies.

By comprehending this captivating illustration, we grasp the incredible reality of how Jesus, our loving Husband Number 2, offers us a new life and empowers us to live according to His expectations. It is a story of redemption, resurrection, and a divine union that liberates us from the clutches of the law, enabling us to experience the abundant life He has prepared for us. Let us embrace the law's message, recognising its purpose in pointing us towards Christ, the ultimate solution to our spiritual needs.

Chapter 8

Jesus Christ: The Restorer of the Living Soul

Forbearance to Perfection through Christ

In the Old Testament, when humanity sinned under the law, a symbolic provision was established to temporarily address the forgiveness of sins. This provision involved the offering of blood from bulls and goats. However, it is important to note that these sacrifices served as a continual reminder of sins, as they lacked the power to permanently cleanse sins, as stated in Hebrews 10:3-5.

These sacrifices of animals could not truly take away sins. In light of this limitation, God had a greater plan in mind. When Christ came into the world, He declared that sacrifices and offerings were not what God desired. Instead, God had prepared a body for Christ to offer as the ultimate sacrifice, as mentioned in Hebrews 10:5.

Under the law, God understood that humans, being in their fleshly state, were incapable of fully fulfilling the spiritual requirements of the law. It was like trying to mix oil and water or unite fire and ice. God, in His wisdom, made allowances and temporary concessions during that time, knowing the limitations of the flesh (the carnal mind), as listed in Galatians 5:19-21.

These works of the flesh, such as adultery, fornication, uncleanness, idolatry, witchcraft, hatred, variance, emulations, wrath, strife, seditions, heresies, envyings, murders, drunkenness, revellings, and similar behaviours, demonstrated the inherent weakness and shortcomings of humanity.

These temporary concessions in the law were given to guide and teach humanity, knowing that they would ultimately fall short. However, God had foreknowledge of the outcome and the capabilities of the flesh. Therefore, these concessions were not meant to be permanent but rather to serve a specific purpose during the period of learning, after which they were abolished.

Some of the concessions made under the law addressed specific issues, such as the first work of the flesh mentioned earlier, which is adultery. If God had not made these concessions, fallen humanity under the law would undoubtedly have engaged in adultery and sought forgiveness by offering sacrifices of bulls and lambs. However, these sacrifices would not have the power to truly take away their sins. As a result, they would repeat the same cycle of sin year after year because they lacked the ability to control themselves due to the inherent nature of sin within them.

Without these concessions, the situation would have been chaotic and destructive, with rampant cases of rape, incest, unwanted pregnancies, broken homes, and infidelity, among other consequences. The damage caused by such sins would have been immense. In order to restrain these excesses, God allowed a concession during that time and permitted the practice of polygamy for those under the law. This permission was limited to the period when they were under the guidance of the schoolmaster, as they were still in the process of learning and growing.

It is important to note that although God's original design for marriage is the union of one man and one woman, polygamy was tolerated in the Old Testament as a temporary measure. Examples of individuals who had multiple wives because of this concession include King David and King Solomon. However, this arrangement was destined to change once the Saviour, the spiritual strength that humanity needed to live righteously, was provided.

Another concession that can be observed is in the area of divorce. In the Gospel of Mark, the Pharisees approached Jesus with a question, asking if it was lawful for a man to divorce his wife. Jesus responded by inquiring about what Moses had commanded regarding this matter. The Pharisees answered that Moses had permitted writing a certificate of divorce and sending the wife away. Jesus then explained to them that Moses had allowed this practice because of the hardness of their hearts, but it was not the original intention from the beginning of creation.

Jesus emphasised that God's original plan was for a man to leave his parents and be joined to his wife, forming a union where the two become one flesh. He firmly stated that what God has joined together, man should not separate. Jesus highlighted that the reason Moses permitted divorce was solely due to the hardness of their hearts, or the stubbornness of their carnal minds.

Even King David, known as a man after God's own heart, struggled with his desires towards women. In his old age, a beautiful young woman named Abishag was brought to him to provide care and comfort. When David did not engage in an intimate relationship with her, it indicated his physical weakness. It is evident that men in the flesh lacked control over sins like adultery, fornication, and lust.

However, amidst this reality, we also encounter individuals like Joseph and Enoch in the Old Testament who stood firm in their commitment to God. Joseph, despite facing repeated temptation from his master's wife, refused to yield, recognising it as a great wickedness and a sin against God. These examples highlight that even in the period of the Law, certain individuals demonstrated unwavering faith and obedience.

As we consider the Old Testament, it is crucial to recognise that if individuals like Joseph and Enoch could stand for God during the time of the Law, which is often referred to as the "Ministration of Death," then how much more should we, who are under the "Ministration of the Spirit," strive to live consistently above sin and manifest the fruit of the Spirit?

Throughout history, God displayed patience and forbearance, overlooking certain acts during the time of man's ignorance. However, with the revelation of the truth, He now commands all people everywhere to repent, to change their old way of thinking, to regret their past sins, and to seek God's purpose for their lives.

It is important to note that God's forbearance in the past does not imply His approval or endorsement of these sins. Rather, it demonstrates His patience and willingness to work with imperfect individuals within the context of their cultural and historical circumstances.

Jesus, the Lamb of God, was predestined to be slain from the foundation of the world. He serves as the ultimate assurance and means of reconciling humanity back to God. The blood of bulls and goats offered in the Old Testament served as temporary provisions, mere placeholders that could not truly take away sins. These sacrifices were but a shadow, a foreshadowing of the good things to come.

The book of Hebrews describes the sacrifices of the law as a shadow of the future reality found in Christ. They were unable to perfect those who came to offer them, for if they could, there would have been no need for them to be continually offered. However, through these sacrifices, there remained a constant reminder of sins, prompting the need for ongoing atonement.

It is the blood of Christ that possesses the true power to save. He is the embodiment of the shadows cast by those symbolic sacrifices. The sacrifices of the law pointed to Christ, who is the substance and fulfilment of those shadows. In Colossians, it is stated that these sacrifices were a mere shadow of things to come, but the reality is found in the body of Christ.

Therefore, it is in Jesus, the perfect sacrifice, that we find redemption and the true cleansing from sin. His sacrifice surpasses the limitations of the temporary and symbolic sacrifices of the Old Testament, providing salvation and eternal reconciliation with God.

The insufficiency of the blood of bulls and goats to save reveals that no one under the law in the Old Testament could be truly saved through those sacrifices, regardless of how many times they were offered. It was precisely for this reason that Jesus died for all, providing salvation for both past sins through God's forbearance and present sins.

In the book of Romans, it is emphasised that the righteousness of God comes through faith in Jesus Christ to all who believe. There is no distinction, for all have sinned and fall short of God's glory. However, through God's grace, they are justified freely by His redemption in Christ Jesus. Jesus has been set forth as a propitiation through faith in His blood, demonstrating God's righteousness in forgiving past sins through His forbearance. This was done to declare His righteousness in the present time, in order for God to be just and the justifier of the one who has faith in Jesus.

The concept of forbearance encompasses God's patient self-control, restraint, and tolerance. God displayed tolerance toward past sins, but through faith in the blood of Jesus shed on the cross, those who lived during the period of God's forbearance can have their sins forgiven and remitted.

Thus, Jesus' sacrifice extends to all humanity, encompassing both those who lived under the law in the Old Testament and those who exist in the present time. Through faith in His blood, individuals can experience the remission of sins and partake in the salvation provided by God's grace and mercy.

God's forbearance with the sins of those under the law is attributed to His desire for repentance. The goodness of God is what leads individuals to repentance, as stated in Romans 2:1-4. It highlights the inexcusability of judging others while being guilty of the same sins. By judging others, one actually condemns themselves, for God's judgment is based on truth and holds those accountable who engage in such actions. It is a fallacy to assume that by judging others, one can escape God's judgment. Instead, individuals should recognise and appreciate the richness of God's goodness, forbearance, and long-suffering. They should understand that despising His goodness and forbearance reflects a lack of awareness that it is God's goodness that actually leads to repentance.

But how can those who died before Jesus was crucified get the opportunity to hear the gospel and make up their minds to accept or reject the offer of Salvation?

Jesus, after His death, preached and saved some individuals who had died. We have already established that the blood of bulls and goats could not take away sins; they only provided temporary purification of the flesh. However, the blood of Jesus, which is the true solution, takes away the sins of the world and purges the conscience from dead works. This is why Jesus's blood was shed as a mediator of the new testament and for the redemption of transgressions under the old testament.

For those who died before Jesus's crucifixion, when He rose from the dead, they were the first beneficiaries of His sacrificial death. He went to preach to those who were dead, and as the judge of both the living and the dead, they were given the opportunity to hear the gospel. The book of 1 Peter 4:5-6 states, "Who shall give account to him that is ready to judge the quick and the dead. For for this cause was the gospel preached also to them that are dead, that they might be judged according to men in the flesh, but live according to God in the spirit."

Scripture provides us with insight into some of these individuals whom Jesus preached to after His death. They include those who perished during the time of Noah's flood. Therefore, not all of them perished, as some had the opportunity to repent after Jesus's crucifixion. 1 Peter 3:18-20 reveals, "For Christ also hath once suffered for sins, the just for the unjust, that he might bring us to God, being put to death in the flesh, but quickened by the Spirit: By which also he went and preached unto the spirits in prison; Which sometime were disobedient, when once the long-suffering of God waited in the days of Noah, while the ark was a preparing, wherein few, that is, eight souls were saved by water."

It is important to understand that the death of Jesus marked a significant shift in God's plan. It served as the dividing line between God's forbearance and His call for all people to repent and strive for perfection. Acts 17:30 emphasises the importance of this transition, stating that God now commands everyone to repent and change their ways.

While those who died before the crucifixion of Christ had the opportunity to hear the gospel and have it preached to their spirits after death, this is no longer the case. It is crucial for individuals everywhere to be born again before they die because there is no opportunity for repentance after death. The next event after death is judgment. This is why the scriptures emphasise that "Today is the day of salvation." (2 Corinthians 6:2)

Likewise, the forbearance of God, which involved overlooking acts of idolatry, allowing polygamy, divorce, and other transgressions, also ended with the death of Jesus. The veil in the temple was torn, signifying the fulfillment of the law by Jesus. He declared, "It is finished," indicating that the penalty for sin had been paid and that the grace that brings salvation had appeared to all people. As a result, no one should have an excuse for not pleasing God or striving for perfection.

In the Old Testament, the law was given with leniency, as it relied on human effort to fulfil it. However, when Jesus came, He declared in Matthew 5:17-18, "Think not that I am come to destroy the law, or the prophets: I am not come to destroy, but to fulfil. For verily I say unto you, Till heaven and earth pass, one jot or one tittle shall in no wise pass from the law, till all be fulfilled." Jesus came to fulfil the law on our behalf so that through faith in Him, we can be counted as righteous and partake in the fulfilment of the law.

Jesus, in Matthew 5:19-20, warns that breaking even the least commandments and teaching others to do the same will result in being called the least in the kingdom of heaven. On the other hand, those who both do and teach the commandments will be called great in the kingdom of heaven. He further states that our righteousness must exceed that of the scribes and Pharisees in order to enter the kingdom of heaven.

In other words, Jesus did not come to abolish the law but to fulfil every aspect of it, down to the smallest details. Teaching against the fulfilment of the law, even in its least parts, brings a curse upon oneself. Instead, the law should be fully fulfilled, and our righteousness under the ministration of the Spirit should surpass that of those under the ministration of death. This aligns with Luke 12:48, which explains that those who have been given much, like the knowledge of the law and grace, will be required to do much more, as they have received greater responsibility.

The forbearance of God was in effect when people sought to please Him through their fleshly efforts. However, now that the grace to please God through the life offered by Jesus Christ is available, more is expected from us. Polygamy and other practices that were overlooked in the past are no longer condoned in the new testament. God now expects us to align ourselves with the price Jesus paid for us and strive for perfection through faith. Our responsibility is to fix our lives and rely on the finished work of Jesus as the author and finisher of our faith. Through this, we will be transformed into His image of perfection and maturity as children of God.

Jesus exemplified how in the new testament dispensation, greater expectations are placed on believers, and we cannot compare ourselves with those under the old testament. In Matthew 5:21-22, Jesus declares that the commandment "You shall not kill" was understood in the past as pertaining to the physical act of killing and the consequence of judgment. However, Jesus goes further and says that even harbouring anger without cause or insulting others puts one in danger of judgment and hellfire. This demonstrates that in the new testament, Jesus addresses the root of sin, not just its outward manifestation.

In the old testament, God showed leniency and forbearance by not immediately counting anger as sin unless it resulted in murder. But in the new testament, purchased by the blood of Jesus, a higher standard is set. Jesus urges believers to be aware of the power of the life in His blood and use it to live a victorious life and strive for the expected perfection.

Matthew 5:17-48 is recommended for new testament believers to study in order to grasp the depth of the perfection Christ expects from every believer. The good news is that we do not have to fulfil these requirements in our own strength. Through our union with Christ as our spiritual Husband, we are released from our previous relationship with the law (Husband 1) and now belong to Jesus (Husband 2), who has fulfilled the law and its demands on our behalf. Our focus should be on nurturing our relationship and fellowship with the Lord Jesus in order to benefit from His accomplishments. Christianity is centred around a personal relationship with Jesus, rather than mere religious observance.

To further emphasise the higher expectations in the new testament, Jesus addresses the issue of adultery in Matthew 15:27-28. He states that while it was previously said not to commit adultery, he now declares that even looking at a woman with lust is already committing adultery in the heart. In the old testament, polygamy was permitted as a concession to curb the excesses of adultery. However, in the new testament, polygamy is abolished because the life of Christ enables us to be perfected, and adultery is addressed at its root. When a person looks at someone with lust, God, who sees the heart, considers it as adultery already committed. This may seem challenging, but the provision of victory through the blood of Jesus makes it possible to fulfil this standard.

Jesus also addresses the topic of divorce, which was allowed by Moses in the old testament. In Matthew 15:31-32, Jesus states that although it was said to give a certificate of divorce, he declares that whoever divorces his wife, except for the cause of fornication, causes her to commit adultery. Additionally, whoever marries a divorced woman also commits adultery.

The conclusion of the matter is found in Matthew 15:48, where Jesus alludes to the expectation of perfection for every believer. He instructs believers to be perfect, just as their heavenly Father is perfect. This highlights the call for believers to strive for perfection in their walk with Christ.

***

The Incarnation of the Son of God

When humanity fell, their spiritual connection was severed, and they were left in a fallen state known as the Flesh, the natural or carnal man. The Bible states, "He that is born of FLESH is FLESH." We never witnessed man in his original spiritual glory because sin entered before the first generation. Thus, we only know the substandard version of man.

Reconciling man with God, who is Spirit, requires bridging the gap between flesh and Spirit. The ideal solution is for a Spirit being, the very source Himself—God—to restore this connection. However, sin presents an obstacle that must be addressed. The consequences of sin need to be fulfilled. To re-establish the connection, a rebirth is necessary using the existing shell.

A Spirit cannot die in place of flesh; it would be unfair. It requires a like-for-like substitution. Therefore, the Spirit being, the Word, had to become flesh. As John 1:14 states, "And the Word was made flesh, and dwelt among us." The Word came in the likeness of sinful flesh, condemning sin in the flesh (Romans 8:3). Yet, Jesus was without sin (1 John 3:5).

Jesus needed to be 100% flesh to be the perfect sacrifice since it was flesh that sinned and the penalty needed to be paid by flesh. If Jesus came as God, it would have been impossible to kill Him, as God is Spirit and cannot die. Additionally, when Herod sought to kill Jesus as a child, angels intervened, guiding Joseph to flee to Egypt and later return to Israel (Matthew 2:13-15, 19-23). None of this would have been necessary if Jesus came as God. Furthermore, angels are ministering spirits to humans, indicating that Jesus, as God, would not have required angelic protection.

Jesus took on various forms. He transitioned from the Word to flesh (Philippians 2:7) and became a servant, disfigured on His way to the cross (Isaiah 53:2-8). He became sin itself (2 Corinthians 5:21) to the extent that God turned away from Him, leading Jesus to cry out, "My God, My God, why have you forsaken me?" (Matthew 27:46). We know that God's eyes are too holy to behold iniquity (Habakkuk 1:13), so when Jesus carried the sin of the world, God had to turn away. However, in the end, Jesus was glorified (Philippians 2:9).

Jesus was made a little lower than the angels (Hebrews 2:9) for the purpose of suffering death, which ultimately led to bringing many sons to glory. Through His sacrificial death, Jesus has reproduced Himself in us, raising more sons through the life He offers (John 12:24). By dying and being resurrected, Jesus brought forth abundant fruit.

Chapter 9

The Rebirth of the Living Soul

The Gift of the Holy Spirit: Restoring the Connection with God's Ruach

Jesus emphasised the importance of rightly dividing the word of truth. When we examine the scriptures, we see that some of the things Jesus said to his disciples were still under the law, although they are classified under the New Testament writings such as Matthew, Mark, Luke, and others. However, the true beginning of the New Testament occurred after Christ's death. Through his sacrificial death, he introduced the New Testament and revealed the personhood of the Godhead to enable us to benefit from the New Testament, which begins with the book of Acts.

Jesus serves as a model for us to follow. As an experiment or prototype, he came to earth as 100% man and was sustained entirely by the Holy Spirit from birth to resurrection. He demonstrated practically how a person can live a victorious life by having koinonia or fellowship with the Holy Spirit. Below are just a few examples of the extraordinary things Jesus accomplished with the aid and power of the Holy Spirit.

1. Conception and Birth: Jesus' conception in the womb of Mary was by the Holy Spirit. The angel Gabriel announced to Mary in Luke 1:35, "The Holy Spirit will come upon you, and the power of the Most High will overshadow you; therefore, the child to be born will be called holy—the Son of God."

2. Baptism: When Jesus was baptized by John the Baptist, the Holy Spirit descended upon Him in the form of a dove. Matthew 3:16 describes the moment, saying, "And when Jesus was baptized, immediately he went up from the water, and behold, the heavens were opened to him, and he saw the Spirit of God descending like a dove and coming to rest on him."

3. Led to the Wilderness: After His baptism, Jesus was led by the Holy Spirit into the wilderness, where He fasted for forty days and was tempted by the devil. This is mentioned in Matthew 4:1: "Then Jesus was led up by the Spirit into the wilderness to be tempted by the devil."

4. Casting out Demons: Jesus performed many miracles, including casting out demons. In Matthew 12:28, Jesus said, "But if it is by the Spirit of God that I cast out demons, then the kingdom of God has come upon you."

5. Resurrection: Jesus' resurrection from the dead was accomplished through the power of the Holy Spirit. Romans 8:11 states, "If the Spirit of him who raised Jesus from the dead dwells in you, he who raised Christ Jesus from the dead will also give life to your mortal bodies through his Spirit who dwells in you."

The Spirit played a crucial role in Jesus' life, ministry, and redemptive work. Just as sin entered the world through one man, Adam, Jesus came as the seed of righteousness to redeem us. In Romans 5:19, it says, "For as by one man's disobedience the many were made sinners, so by one man's obedience the many will be made righteous." Jesus' obedience to the Father, empowered by the Holy Spirit, made it possible for us to be reconciled to God.

Jesus understood that His life was not meant for Himself alone, so just as a grain of wheat must fall to the earth and die to multiply, Jesus' death on the cross became the source of life for many sons and daughters of God. In John 12:24, Jesus said, "Truly, truly, I say to you, unless a grain of wheat falls into the earth and dies, it remains alone; but if it dies, it bears much fruit."

Jesus' sacrifice opened the way for fallen humanity to have a ray of hope and the opportunity to be reconciled to God. In John 15:13, He said, "Greater love has no one than this, that someone lay down his life for his friends." Jesus willingly laid down His life on the cross, making His life available as a seed of righteousness for us to receive and be reconciled to God.

After His death and resurrection, Jesus knew that there was a need for the distribution of this seed of life to be made available to all people. He promised the coming of the Holy Spirit as the implementer and distributor of this life. In John 16:7, Jesus said, "Nevertheless, I tell you the truth: it is to your advantage that I go away, for if I do not go away, the Helper will not come to you. But if I go, I will send him to you."

The Holy Spirit, also known as the life-giving Spirit, is the medium of distribution for the life of Christ. In Romans 8:11, it states, "If the Spirit of him who raised Jesus from the dead dwells in you, he who raised Christ Jesus from the dead will also give life to your mortal bodies through his Spirit who dwells in you." Through the Holy Spirit, the same power that raised Jesus from the dead is made available to us, enabling us to live victorious lives.

***

Dispensation of the Life of Christ: Flowing from Spirit to Body

Below is a detailed explanation of how the Holy Spirit works in us to distribute the life of Christ by using the triune structure of man.

1. Spirit giving life to the soul: When God breathed His spirit of life (ruach) into the body of man formed from the dust of the earth at creation, man became a living soul (Genesis 2:7). The union of the spirit and the body gave birth to the soul, and it is the spirit that gives life to the soul. However, when man sinned, God withdrew His spirit, and the soul of man died. But through redemption, Jesus sent us the Holy Spirit, who is referred to as the "life-giving" spirit (1 Corinthians 15:45). The Holy Spirit supplies life to our soul, bringing it back to life. Illustration: Think of a lamp that requires electricity to shine. The lamp represents our soul, and the electricity represents the life-giving Spirit. Without

electricity, the lamp cannot emit light. Similarly, without the Holy Spirit, our soul remains lifeless. But when the Holy Spirit fills our soul, it comes alive, reflecting the light of God's presence.

2. The soul as the medium of communication: The soul is meant to mirror the spirit, and the body mirrors the soul. However, a spirit cannot directly interface with flesh, as they are contrary to each other (Galatians 5:17). Therefore, the soul acts as the medium of communication, serving as the interpreter between the spirit and the body. It is through the soul that the spirit imparts its influence and direction to the body.

3. Receiving the Holy Spirit and the soul's role: At salvation, when we receive the Holy Spirit, we receive His fullness in our spirit. It is important to note that the Holy Spirit is a personality that cannot be depleted. While our spirit is joined with the Spirit of God in His fullness, we are expected to yield our soul to the Holy Spirit. He pours out from our spirit into our soul, which is like a cup. Depending on our level of yielding to the Holy Spirit, we can receive measures or an overflow of the Spirit. Illustration: Imagine a pitcher pouring water into a cup. The pitcher represents the Holy Spirit, and the cup represents our soul. The more we yield to the Holy Spirit, the more He fills our soul. The content of our soul then influences the behaviour of our physical body. Just as the state of the cup determines how much water it can hold, the state of our soul determines the measure of the Holy Spirit's influence and manifestation in our lives.

4. Interdependence of the Trinity and its parallel to the Spirit, soul, and body: The interdependent relationship within the triune Godhead (Father, Son, and Holy Spirit) mirrors the interdependence of the spirit, soul, and body. The Holy Spirit does not speak of Himself but waits for Jesus to reveal Himself to us (John 16:13-14). Similarly, Jesus does not speak of Himself but glorifies and does what He sees the Father doing (John 8:28; John 14:10). This interdependence within the Godhead is a model for the interplay between our spirit, soul, and body.

Illustration: Consider a relay race where three runners pass the baton to one another. The first runner represents the Holy Spirit, who reveals Jesus (the second runner). Jesus, in turn, reveals the Father (the third runner). The baton symbolizes the revelation and manifestation of God's nature and purposes. Just as the runners depend on one another to complete the race, our spirit, soul, and body rely on each other for the full expression and experience of God's divine life.

***

The Three Stages of Salvation

Man is a triune being, consisting of spirit, soul, and body. In the same way, salvation, the offer of eternal life through the Spirit, also occurs in three stages.

Just as death has three stages, salvation follows a similar pattern. The first stage of death is spiritual death, which occurs instantly. This is the separation of the spirit from God, leading to spiritual decay and separation from His life-giving presence. The second stage is the progressive death of the soul, which includes the withering of the soul due to sin and its consequences. Lastly, the third stage is the death of the physical body, which occurs when it succumbs to corruption and returns to the dust from which it came.

Likewise, salvation is a process that unfolds in three stages. These stages involve the redemption and restoration of the spirit, soul, and body of the believer, bringing them into fullness of life and fellowship with God. Just as death had its progression, salvation also has a journey that leads to the ultimate transformation and eternal life in Christ.

1. Salvation of the Spirit: This is a profound and instantaneous transformation that occurs when we become born again. It is similar to the immediate change in status when two individuals enter into a marriage covenant. Just as the Scripture declares, "He that is joined to the Lord is one spirit" (1 Corinthians 6:17).

When a couple exchanges vows and enters into the covenant of marriage, their status changes in an instant. They are no longer two separate individuals but are united as one. Similarly, when we accept Jesus Christ as our Saviour and Lord, confessing our sins and repenting, our spirit experiences an immediate union with the Spirit of the Lord.

This truth is beautifully captured in the Scripture's description of our new identity in Christ. It states, "Therefore, if anyone is in Christ, he is a new creation; old things have passed away; behold, all things have become new" (2 Corinthians 5:17). Just as marriage brings about a new legal and relational status, our union with Christ brings about a profound and immediate transformation at the core of our being.

In this spiritual union, our old nature, separated from God by sin, is replaced by a new nature that is connected to the life-giving Spirit of God. Our spirit, once dead in sin, is now alive and united with the Spirit of the Lord. This instantaneous change is similar to the declaration of marriage vows, where two individuals are declared husband and wife in an instant.

Just as a married couple begins a lifelong journey together, the salvation of our spirit marks the beginning of our lifelong journey of faith. It is the foundation upon which we build our relationship with God and experience His transformative work in our lives. As we grow in our understanding of this union with Christ, we align our thoughts, emotions, and actions with the truth of His Word, reflecting His character and love. This process of aligning our soul with the saved spirit is described as the next stage of salvation.

2. Salvation of the Soul: This is a transformative journey in which we align our thoughts, emotions, and actions with the truth of God's Word, leading us to progressively become more like Christ in our character and conduct.

The salvation of the soul is the ongoing work of the Holy Spirit within us, made possible by the new spirit that resides in us. It is through this indwelling Spirit that our minds are transformed as we yield to His influence. The Word of God plays a crucial role in this process, as it serves as a cleansing agent for our minds. As the Scripture says, "You are already clean because of the word which I have spoken to you" (John 15:3). The Word of God washes and purifies our thoughts, aligning them with the truth.

It is important to recognise that the Holy Spirit not only works in us but also works through us. He is the one who enables us to desire and carry out God's good pleasure. As the Scripture declares, "For it is God who works in you both to will and to do for His good pleasure" (Philippians 2:13). However, we have an active role to play in this process. We are called to work out, or exhibit, the workings of the Spirit in our lives. Jesus Himself acknowledged the weakness of our flesh, saying, "The spirit is willing, but the flesh is weak" (Matthew 26:41). Therefore, as believers, we continually rely on the strength and guidance of the Holy Spirit to manifest His work in and through us.

Furthermore, the Holy Spirit has distributed spiritual gifts to believers for the purpose of perfecting the saints and building up the body of Christ. These gifts are meant to be utilised within the context of the assembly of believers. The Scripture admonishes us not to forsake the gathering of believers, as it is within this community that we bring our gifts together, completing the puzzle and sharpening one another. As it is written, "And let us consider one another in order to stir up love and good works, not forsaking the assembling of ourselves together, as is the manner of some, but exhorting one another..." (Hebrews 10:24-25). In this collective setting, as we hear the Word of God from pastors, apostles, evangelists, and other members, our minds are further perfected, and faith is birthed within us through the hearing of the Word.

Through the continuous washing of water by the Word of God, our souls receive salvation. We are progressively sanctified and set apart for God's purposes, and our minds are renewed. As a result, we are transformed, becoming holy without spot or wrinkle, and our affections are set on heavenly things. This process of salvation of the soul leads us to attain the full stature of Christ as we grow in spiritual maturity and reflect His character in increasing measure.

3.   Salvation of the Body: This is a process that involves managing and subduing the corrupt nature of the flesh. Our bodies are subject to corruption, and even while we are alive, the flesh continues to make its demands known. The apostle Paul acknowledged the fallen state of the flesh, declaring that nothing good dwells in it (Romans 7:18). The flesh manifests its desires through the lust of the eyes, the lust of the flesh, and the pride of life (1 John 2:16).

To navigate this challenge, we are called to manage and crucify the body daily. Paul admonishes us to keep our bodies under control and not to make provisions for the flesh to fulfil its lusts (1 Corinthians 9:27; Romans 13:14). Just as Jesus taught, if we desire to follow His example of crucifixion, we must take up our cross daily and deny the carnal nature, along with its demands and the influence of the five senses (Luke 9:23).

By managing the body in this manner, we can experience daily victory over sin and its demands. However, we must remain watchful, recognising that any area of the body's corrupt nature that has not been brought under control becomes a loophole for the devil to tempt and lead us into compromise. Therefore, it is a continuous process of partnering with the Holy Spirit to subdue the body and live in righteousness. However, the ultimate salvation of the body occurs when, as Paul explains, we are changed. This corruptible body will put on corruption, and this mortal body will put on immortality (1 Corinthians 15:53). This transformation of the body can only be fully realized through death or the rapture, when believers will receive their glorified bodies, free from corruption and imperfection.

Chapter 10

Bearing the Image of Adam

Beholding as in a mirror

To bear the image of the last Adam means to resemble Him, and this is not a promise reserved for the future. Similarly, the promise of eternal life for believers is not solely for the afterlife; it begins at the moment of salvation. As Christians, we are called to bear the image of the last Adam as our identity. 1 Corinthians 15:49 (NLT) affirms this by stating, "Just as we are now like the earthly man, we will someday be like the heavenly man."

It is crucial to bear the image of the last Adam because, through this, fallen man, who had taken on the image of the first Adam and lost his resemblance to God, is reconciled to his original design in the image of God. However, bearing the image of the last Adam requires a process of beholding. To behold means to see, look upon, or gaze at. The continuous form of behold is beholding, indicating an ongoing and consistent practice.

Jesus, the author and perfecter of our faith, is mentioned in Hebrews 12:2, which encourages us to "look unto Jesus." Looking or beholding implies a continuous process, and it is through engaging in this process that we begin to experience the transformative power of the cross and achieve the ultimate goal of becoming like Jesus, the last Adam. 2 Corinthians 3:18 explains that "as we are beholding the glory of the Lord, we are being transformed into the same image from glory to glory, just as by the Spirit of the Lord."

Transformation into the likeness of the last Adam is not an automatic process like it was with the first Adam before his fall. The first Adam was created as a fully grown man with the breath of life (ruach) within him, which gave birth to a living soul. He was an explicit image of God in His likeness. However, when man fell, he fell short of his original glory, the glory of God. God took His Spirit from man, and man became flesh, returning to the dust—a natural man.

To restore man to God, the Spirit of God that departed during the fall needed to be reintroduced. Therefore, the last Adam had to be God Himself, "the Lord from heaven," for God is Spirit. Hence, 1 Corinthians 15:46 states, "However, the spiritual is not first, but the natural, and afterward the spiritual," indicating the order of birth. It is essential to note that the first birth occurred after the fall of man. Adam and Eve were not born but were created as fully grown adults, and they had already disobeyed God and fallen before their first child, Cain, was born. Thus, everyone born after them has never experienced life before the fall, and our default position has been the natural fallen state of man. Therefore, when we speak of a second birth, it is a spiritual birth that enables us to taste the original image our forefather Adam experienced before sin.

When the last Adam came, He entered through the established process of human reproduction, being born as a baby and growing into adulthood. Anything born as a baby, not a fully grown adult, is expected to grow. Thus, the transformation into the likeness of the last Adam begins at the moment of spiritual birth.

Considering that we have all been naturally born into a sinful world in our fleshly state, the process of reconciliation also begins with a birth—the spiritual birth of being born again. This truth is exemplified in John 3:3, where Jesus addressed Nicodemus, a Jewish ruler, and declared, "Unless one is born again, he cannot see the kingdom of God." Nicodemus, perplexed by this statement, questioned in verse 4, "How can a man be born when he is old? Can he enter a second time into his mother's womb and be born?" Nicodemus struggled to comprehend the concept of being born again. Jesus clarified His point in verse 5, saying, "Unless one is born of water and the Spirit, he cannot enter the kingdom of God." Here, Jesus made it clear that He was not referring to a physical birth but a spiritual one. John 3:6 clarifies this by stating, "That which is born of the flesh is flesh, and that which is born of the Spirit is spirit." If we substitute the terms "First Adam" for "flesh" and "Last Adam" for "spirit" in the text, it reads, "That which is born of the First Adam is flesh, and that which is born of the Last Adam is spirit." Hence, Jesus alleviated Nicodemus's confusion and told him in verse 7, "Do not marvel that I said to you, 'You must be born again.'"

***

The Process of Spiritual Growth and Transformation

Just as natural babies require growth, so do spiritual babies. In 1 Peter 2:2, it is written, "As newborn babes, desire the pure milk of the word, that you may grow thereby." Unlike the first Adam, who was not born and therefore did not need to grow, every person born after Adam must go through a growth process. However, this process of growth is not a simple or quick endeavour. It requires time, patience, and a commitment to the journey.

As newborn babes in Christ, our growth may initially seem challenging because we were accustomed to the old life of the flesh, which enticed us with the allure of instant and speedy gratification. We were like people who preferred the taste of old wine, believing that the older was better (Luke 5:39). But now, as we embrace the new life of the spirit, we come to realise that its results may not be immediate or readily apparent. It requires patience, perseverance, and faith to continue on this path of spiritual growth. We may face moments of doubt and frustration and be tempted to abandon the process because the old ways seem more appealing.

However, let us not forget the words of Jesus in Luke 5:39: "No man also, having drunk old wine straightway, desireth new; for he saith, The old is better." These words caution us against the inclination to cling to the familiar and comfortable, even when we know deep down that there is something greater awaiting us.

To illustrate this, let us consider the concept of instant gratification through junk food. When we consume sugary treats like chocolates and sweets, we may experience a quick sugar rush that makes us feel bubbly and active almost immediately. It provides instant energy and momentarily satisfies our cravings. In contrast, when we choose to eat healthily, incorporating greens and vegetables into our diet, we may not experience an instant energy boost. It may feel like the process is not working, tempting us to abandon it altogether.

However, if we stay the course and remain committed to eating healthily, something remarkable happens. Over time, our bodies become stronger and healthier, with lasting effects. The choice to nourish ourselves with nutritious foods builds a solid foundation for our well-being. It is a process that requires discipline and patience, but the long-term benefits far outweigh the fleeting satisfaction of junk food.

In the same way, the lust of the flesh can be likened to the allure of junk food. It offers immediate gratification and promises quick results. However, the life that the spirit offers is akin to choosing to eat healthily. It may not provide instant gratification or immediate visible changes, but it nurtures our spiritual well-being and leads to lasting growth.

It is crucial to understand that growth in the spirit takes time and perseverance. Just as healthy eating builds a solid structure for our physical bodies, embracing the life of the spirit nurtures our spiritual growth and development. By resisting the temptation of instant gratification and staying committed to the process, we can experience true transformation and a deepening connection with God. Remember, nothing good comes easy, and the rewards of spiritual growth are worth the investment of time and effort.

As babies grow, they encounter setbacks, stress, adversity, failure, challenges, and even trauma. When they learn to walk, they stumble and fall, sometimes experiencing great discomfort. They may cry, but they gather the strength to rise again and continue learning. This ability to overcome challenges and cope with stress is known as resilience. Resilience is not something that children either possess or lack; it is a skill that develops as they grow. Similarly, spiritual infants need to grow and cultivate spiritual resilience.

This spiritual resilience is described as a right or power in John 1:12, which states, "But as many as received Him, to them He gave the right (power, KJV) to become children of God, to those who believe in His name." This right or power is bestowed upon those who are born again, not through blood, the will of the flesh, or the will of man, but through God.

Just as physical resilience is developed through growth, this spiritual right or power is also a skill that spiritual children develop as they mature. Our growth process is transformative as we behold Jesus and gradually become like Him in His image. However, this transformation is made possible through the work of the Holy Spirit.

Unlike the first Adam, who was created in the image of God without needing a growth process, we are born as spiritual infants. Our ultimate aim is to grow into maturity, which is characterized by sonship, or being fully conformed to the image of God. This requires our active participation, as we are not born fully developed. We enter into the process of growth, becoming the same image as God through the work of His Spirit, who has birthed us into this journey.

***

Active Participation in the Process of Restoration

We can compare the process of reconciliation and restoration to the incident involving Moses and the tablets of the Ten Commandments. Initially, God gave Moses the completed tablets, already carved and inscribed with the commandments by God's own finger (Exodus 31:18). Moses played no role in their creation other than receiving them as a finished product, a testimony of God's law.

Similarly, just as Adam sinned and fell short of God's glory, Moses became angry and broke the tablets of the commandments when he witnessed the Israelites worshipping a golden calf (Exodus 32:19). Whether it is sin or anger, anything contrary to God's will does not produce good outcomes, regardless of the cause. In Adam's case, it was the deception of the serpent, while in Moses's case, it was the idolatry of the Israelites that provoked his anger.

When God observed the people's stiff necks and desired to destroy them, He told Moses in Exodus 32:10, "Now therefore, let Me alone, that My wrath may burn hot against them and I may consume them. And I will make of you a great nation." However, Moses did not leave God alone but interceded on behalf of the people (Exodus 32:11–14). Little did Moses know that he could not be more compassionate than God Himself. The very people for whom he pleaded and whose actions led to his anger in breaking the tablets were the same people who would cause his anger once again, resulting in his death and his inability to enter the promised land (Exodus 20:10–12).

After the incident with the golden calf, God instructs Moses to prepare new tablets, marking the first step of Moses's involvement in the restoration of the broken tablets to their original state. God promises to write the same words on the new tablets as were on the first ones that Moses had broken. Exodus 34:1 (ESV) records God's words to Moses: "The Lord said to Moses, 'Cut for yourself two tablets of stone like the first, and I will write on the tablets the words that were on the first tablets, which you broke.'"

At this point, Moses did not know the extent of his involvement, but resilience, right, or power were necessary as the growth process takes time. Patience and consistency are required to reach the desired outcome. Reconciliation or restoration may not come easily but will require your participation.

In Matthew 11:28, Jesus invites all who labour and are burdened to come to Him, promising to give them rest. However, this rest that Jesus offers does not come without our participation in the process. Jesus goes on to say in verse 29, "Take my yoke upon you, and learn from me, for I am gentle and lowly in heart, and you will find rest for your souls."

Why does Jesus emphasise learning from Him? It is because He exemplifies meekness and humility. He willingly laid down His divinity to take on humanity, ultimately sacrificing Himself for the sake of our salvation and overcoming death. This great sacrifice led to His glorification.

Likewise, our salvation and restoration require our active involvement. We are called to work it out, which involves the external expression of what is happening inside of us. God has promised to rewrite His law upon our hearts

(Jeremiah 31:33), transforming us from the inside out. However, it requires our active participation and cooperation. We are called to seek His presence, learn from Him, and obediently follow His ways.

The process of rewriting the law within us involves aligning our thoughts, attitudes, and actions with God's truth. As we yield ourselves to His guidance and surrender our lives to His will, we actively participate in the work of transformation that God is accomplishing within us. We partner with God, who provides the willingness and empowers us to do His good pleasure. Philippians 2:13 states, "Work out your own salvation with fear and trembling, for it is God who works in you, both to will and to work for his good pleasure."

Moses had to learn to partner with God. He spent forty days and forty nights in fellowship with God, beholding His presence, in order to receive the commandments directly from God. Unlike before, this time Moses would write them with his own hands instead of God writing them with His finger. Exodus 34:27-28 (ESV) states: "And the Lord said to Moses, 'Write these words, for in accordance with these words I have made a covenant with you and with Israel.' So he was there with the Lord forty days and forty nights. He neither ate bread nor drank water. And he wrote on the tablets the words of the covenant, the Ten Commandments."

Thus, we observe the sequence of events in which God initially wrote the commandments on the tablets, Moses broke them in anger, and then Moses wrote the commandments again on new tablets as instructed by God. Similarly, God created Adam in His image and likeness, Adam sinned and fell short of God's glory, and then God birthed the Last Adam who had to die (John 12:23-24) and sent us the same Spirit (John 16:7) that raised Him from the dead (Romans 8:11). Through this same Spirit, received at salvation, we have the opportunity to write His Word on the tablets of our hearts (Hebrews 10:15-16; 2 Corinthians 3:2-6) if we submit ourselves to the process (Romans 6:16). In doing so, many sons are brought to glory (Hebrews 2:10).

The process of rewriting the Ten Commandments by Moses provides us with a valuable lesson. While it may have taken little or no time for God to write the commandments initially, Moses, in his involvement, spent forty days and forty nights rewriting them on new stone tablets. This highlights the importance of our participation and the time required for the reconciliation of man to the Image of God.

In the garden of Eden, God created man in His own image in a day. However, the restoration of this image in us necessitates our involvement and takes time to complete the process. Sadly, many believers fall short of attaining the full stature of the fullness of Christ. They mistakenly believe that a simple confession of faith or the sinner's prayer should instantly transform them into the Image of God and enable them to live victorious lives over sin.

As a result, they often become discouraged when they find themselves still struggling with hidden sins even after their salvation experience. They may repeatedly recite the sinner's prayer, engage in deliverance services, or embark on fasting and prayer, longing to experience the abundant life promised in Christ and reflect His Image. However, they fail to realise that salvation is just the beginning of a transformative process.

In John 1:12, we learn that receiving Jesus grants us the right or power to become children of God. This indicates that the journey toward becoming the Image of God requires our active participation. It is not an instantaneous event but a progressive transformation that takes place over time.

Jesus has provided us with various resources to help us in this process of perfection. Ephesians 4:13 speaks of attaining the measure of the stature of the fullness of Christ, which is the perfect man. However, this attainment requires our engagement and willingness to walk in obedience and alignment with God's Word.

To fully grasp the concepts of freedom from sin, the ongoing struggle with sin, and the process of becoming the Image of God, let us consider an illustration using the story of Takwana and a kind and loving counsellor. Takwana was enslaved to a harmful substance and if caught is due a hefty penalty for the abuse of drugs. Takwana, unfortunately, hasn't got the means to pay the penalty and is helpless in overcoming this addiction by herself. The counsellor, who was also wealthy, approached the government to pay all the penalties for drug offenders but the government agreed to this, on the condition that the offenders enter a rehabilitation program and cease their engagement with harmful substances. The counsellor accepts this condition and makes the payment, but the challenge lies in convincing the drug addicts to sign up and participate in the program.

Takwana, desperate for help, encountered the kind and loving counsellor who offered assistance in overcoming her addiction. Takwana accepted and entered the rehabilitation program.

In this illustration:

· Takwana's decision to seek help represents turning to Jesus and accepting His sacrifice on the cross.

· The counsellor represents Jesus, who offers forgiveness, salvation, and freedom from the penalty of sin.

· The rehabilitation program symbolises the process of sanctification, where Takwana embarks on the journey of overcoming addiction and breaking free from its control.

After Takwana's decision to enter the rehabilitation program, signifying her faith in Christ, she is no longer bound by the legal consequences of her addiction. She is forgiven and given a fresh start, representing the positional aspect of salvation, where believers are declared righteous before God.

However, despite being legally free from her addiction, Takwana still faces the daily struggle of overcoming her desires and tendencies toward the substance. There are times when she stumbles and gives in to temptation, despite her genuine desire to be free. This mirrors the ongoing struggle with sin that believers experience in their lives.

Takwana's journey toward freedom is a process that requires active engagement in the rehabilitation program, seeking support from the counsellor, and making choices aligned with the desire to overcome addiction. Similarly, believers are called to actively pursue a relationship with God, relying on His grace and strength, and making choices that align with the desire to live a life pleasing to Him.

This illustration helps us understand the positional and progressive aspects of salvation. Takwana's acceptance of help frees her from the legal consequences of addiction, but the ongoing struggle and growth toward complete freedom demand active participation and reliance on the resources provided in the rehabilitation program. Likewise, through Jesus' sacrifice, believers are positioned as forgiven and righteous before God, but the process of sanctification involves continuous growth, reliance on God's grace, and active participation in the Christian journey.

The aim of the rehabilitation program is to transform Takwana into a new person, no longer struggling with desires and tendencies toward the substance, allowing her to be reintroduced to society as a clean individual. Similarly, the goal of the ongoing growth process for believers is not to remain in rehabilitation forever but to learn to live a life free from sin. As believers mature and become the Image of Christ (Sonship), the counsellor is confident in discharging them from the rehabilitation program because they have learned to walk free from sin. However, the counsellor trusts that due to the believer's maturity, they will remain dependent on receiving the right advice that informs their walk, as a relationship and fellowship have been built with the counsellor. Paul expresses this in Galatians 5:16, saying, "I say then: Walk in the Spirit, and you shall not fulfil the lust of the flesh." And in Galatians 5:25, he adds, "If we live in the Spirit, let us also walk in the Spirit." The aim is not merely to live and remain in the rehabilitation centre, but to grow to maturity, so we begin to walk. We know we have attained maturity (sonship) when our walk is led and directed by the counsellor. As Romans 8:14 states, "For as many as are led by the Spirit of God, these are sons of God."

***

The Journey of Sanctification: Complementing Salvation for Spiritual Maturity and Victory Over Sin

Salvation is a magnificent gift that God offers to humanity through Jesus Christ. By accepting His payment for our sins, we are granted access into His kingdom. However, the journey doesn't end there. While salvation delivers us from the legal consequences of sin, it does not immediately eradicate the control or urge to sin within us. To experience spiritual maturity and victory over sin, we need to understand the importance of sanctification. Let us explore how sanctification complements salvation and enables us to quench our hunger for sin by engaging in the nourishing meal of God's Word.

Salvation (Accepting the Payment): Imagine a hungry person who receives a payment for a meal. This payment represents salvation, where Jesus gave Himself as payment for our sins. Through His sacrifice, the legal penalty of sin is covered, and we gain access to the kingdom of God, just as the hungry person gains access to the restaurant where his meal has been paid for.

Sanctification (Engaging in the Meal): Accepting the payment for the meal is not enough to satisfy our hunger. Similarly, stopping at salvation does not automatically free us from the control and urge of sin. Sanctification is the process of taking the meal and actively engaging in it. It is through sanctification that we find victory over sin and grow in spiritual maturity.

Jesus, in His love for the Church, continues to sanctify and purify us. Ephesians 5:25–26 (ESV) says, "Husbands, love your wives, as Christ loved the church and gave himself up for her, that he might sanctify her, having cleansed her by the washing of water with the word." Jesus not only paid the price for our sins but also provided the means for our sanctification—the Word of God.

The Word of God (Nourishing Our Souls): Just as a meal satisfies our physical hunger, the Word of God nourishes our souls and quenches our hunger for sin. When we actively engage with the Scriptures, meditate on them, and apply them to our lives, the process of sanctification unfolds. The Bible is filled with spiritual food that enables us to grow in holiness and purity.

Hebrews 4:12 (ESV) describes the power of God's Word: "For the word of God is living and active, sharper than any two-edged sword, piercing to the division of soul and of spirit, of joints and of marrow, and discerning the thoughts and intentions of the heart." As we allow the Word to penetrate our hearts and minds, it exposes our sinful desires, enabling us to overcome them and live victoriously.

The Transformational Journey: Through sanctification, our hunger for sin diminishes, and we gain spiritual enablement to live above its control. This journey requires our active participation as we allow the truth of God's Word to shape and transform us. The Holy Spirit works within us, using the Word to renew our minds and conform us to the image of Christ.

Ephesians 5:27 (ESV) beautifully depicts the outcome of this sanctifying process: "so that he might present the church to himself in splendour, without spot or wrinkle or any such thing, that she might be holy and without blemish." Through sanctification, we attain holiness and purity, reflecting the character of our Saviour.

Salvation is the starting point of our relationship with God, but sanctification is the ongoing journey that complements and completes our spiritual maturity and victory over sin. Just as a hungry person needs to actively engage in collecting and eating the meal provided, we are called to participate in sanctification by immersing ourselves in the Word of God. As we feed on the Scriptures, our appetite for sin diminishes, and we experience the transformative power of God's truth in our lives. Let us embrace the process of sanctification and allow God to continually shape us into His likeness, experiencing the fullness of spiritual maturity and victory over sin.

***

The Journey of Transformation: Becoming Like Christ

Jesus, the Last Adam, came to fulfill the divine purpose of making us like Him. He accomplished this by living out the possibility of a perfect life, from infancy to adulthood, under the guidance and power of the Holy Spirit. In His great love for us, Jesus made the decision to give His life so that we, His friends, could partake in His divine nature and become like Him. This transformation is a spiritual process, and thus, Jesus bestowed upon us the Holy Spirit as our Helper, leading us towards attaining His image.

When we accept Jesus as our Saviour, our spirit is instantly saved, and we are made new creatures. Our old selves are crucified with Him, and we are raised to newness of life (Romans 6:6; 2 Corinthians 5:17). In this salvation, we receive the fullness of Christ. As the Scriptures testify, "Of His fullness we have all received" (John 1:16).

However, experiencing the fullness of becoming like Christ requires our active engagement. Jesus Himself declared that we must make up our minds to attain the full stature of Christ (Ephesians 4:13). It is not a passive process but one that demands our intentional participation and commitment.

Our minds, or hearts, play a vital role in this transformative journey. Proverbs 23:26 admonishes us, saying, "My son, give me your heart," emphasizing the need for wholehearted surrender to God. When we fully yield our hearts and minds to Him, aligning our will with His, we open ourselves to His transforming work in us.

Additionally, our hunger and thirst for righteousness are instrumental in this process. Jesus proclaimed, "Blessed are those who hunger and thirst for righteousness, for they shall be filled" (Matthew 5:6). This hunger and thirst create a deep longing within us, propelling us towards a deeper relationship with Christ and a desire to be conformed to His likeness.

In the natural realm, when a person determines in their mind to achieve something, they can accomplish what they set out to do. Similarly, in the spiritual realm, our transformation into Christlikeness is heavily reliant on our mind, or heart. This is why the Bible admonishes us to give our hearts to God, recognizing that although Jesus has made His life and the Holy Spirit available to us, our becoming like Christ is dependent on our hunger for it. As the Scriptures declare, "Blessed are those who hunger and thirst for righteousness, for they shall be filled."

The mind plays a crucial role in the transformation process. It is the conduit through which the raw ingredients of our lives can be transformed into the finished product of Christlikeness. Jesus has given us the seed of His life, but just like a farmer, we must make up our minds to actively engage in the process of sowing that seed. This is why Jesus encourages us to "sow to the Spirit and not the flesh" (Galatians 6:8). It requires our intentional involvement and commitment.

Becoming like Christ necessitates our participation. In the natural realm, the Bible warns that laziness and lack of effort lead to poverty (Proverbs 24:30-34). Likewise, in the spiritual realm, those who merely observe and make excuses without taking action will not experience the fullness of Christ's likeness. The Scriptures even state that "he who does not work should not eat" (2 Thessalonians 3:10). This emphasizes the importance of actively engaging in the process of transformation and not being complacent.

Many Christians rightly believe that Jesus has paid the ultimate price for our salvation. However, it is important to understand that although Jesus gave His all, receiving all that He has made available to us requires an engaged mind. The grace for salvation, which grants us entry into the kingdom, has appeared to all people. Yet, the grace for success and advancement in the kingdom is obtained through active involvement. This is why the Scripture tells us that God resists the proud but gives grace to the humble. Jesus exemplified this truth through His willingness to be slain. The Bible declares, "Worthy is the Lamb who was slain to receive glory, honour, power, and riches." This demonstrates that even Jesus Himself had to participate in the process of sacrifice and endure the sufferings of the cross in order to receive the benefits that were promised.

The heart and mind, often used interchangeably, play a pivotal role in achieving our ultimate goal. As the Scriptures proclaim, "As a man thinks in his heart, so is he." Our thoughts and mindset shape our identity and determine the course of our lives. While Jesus has paid the price to bring us into the kingdom, our hearts and minds must be actively engaged for us to grow into sonship and access the full benefits of the kingdom. It is our responsibility to submit our minds to the transformative process. As the apostle Paul urged, "Be transformed by the renewing of your mind." This implies that our minds need to undergo a process of renewal and alignment with the truth of God's Word.

When we speak of engaging or submitting our minds to the process, it is crucial to understand the nature of this mind. Scripture reveals to us the mind we should possess, saying, "Let this mind be in you, which was also in Christ Jesus."

So, what kind of mind did Christ have? It was a mind of humility, submission, and sacrifice, as beautifully portrayed in Philippians 2:5-10. Christ exemplified humility and willingly submitted Himself to the sacrificial journey for our sake.

When we embrace a mind of humility that is willing to engage in the sacrificial path of Christ, we begin to experience the benefits of His work. As the saying goes, "No pain, no gain." Jesus left us with an example of glorification through suffering, and He encourages us to follow in His footsteps. He said, "If anyone desires to come after Me, let him deny himself, take up his cross daily, and follow Me." This indicates that Christ desires our active participation in His suffering in order to achieve the same glorification that He attained.

In essence, we are called to adopt the same mindset of humility, submission, and sacrifice that Christ demonstrated. By embracing His suffering and participating in it, we can experience the ultimate glorification that awaits us. Just as Jesus willingly endured the cross for the joy set before Him, we too must be willing to endure hardships and sacrifices for the sake of our spiritual growth and ultimate glorification.

God, in His divine power, has the ability to call into existence things that do not yet exist. He declares the end from the beginning, unveiling His ultimate plan. However, this does not negate the importance of the process. When the Bible declares that we are heirs and joint-heirs with Christ, it signifies our potential to become like Him. Yet it is accompanied by the condition that we must also share in His sufferings in order to be glorified together with Him.

Although Jesus has already paid the ultimate price for us, He desires our active participation in the process of becoming like Him. This is evident in His exhortation for us to be "doers of the word." Being a doer means allowing the transformative power of the Word to work within us, and we play a crucial role by engaging our minds and outwardly expressing the inner workings of the Holy Spirit within us.

The Bible encourages us to "work out our salvation with trembling and fear," acknowledging that it is God who works in us, providing the willingness and ability to do His will. While God empowers us, we have the responsibility to put that empowerment into action and actively participate in our own transformation.

If we neglect to work out our salvation or fail to be doers of the Word, the Scriptures liken us to someone who looks in a mirror and immediately forgets what they look like. This emphasizes the need for consistency. We are not called to merely glance at the mirror occasionally; rather, we are urged to continuously behold Jesus as if we were gazing into a mirror. It is through this steadfast focus on Christ that we are progressively transformed into His likeness, ultimately becoming sons of God and bearing the image of the Last Adam.

When we embark on the journey of becoming like Christ, it is crucial to engage our minds in the sacrificial process. This path is not without its challenges, but we must persevere, just as Jesus did. Jesus did not focus on the pain, suffering, or sacrifice of the cross. Instead, He set His gaze upon the ultimate goal and the benefits that awaited Him through His sacrifice. The Bible reveals that it was for the joy set before Him that He endured the cross. It is evident that Jesus did not find pleasure in the process itself, but He was able to endure it because His mind was fixed on the final outcome.

Likewise, we are encouraged to adopt the same mindset that was in Christ Jesus. Regardless of how difficult our Christian journey may be, let the goal of becoming like Christ motivate us to set our minds to endure present sufferings. By doing so, we can attain the perfection that God intended for us. The end goal is to attain the perfect image of Christ as Paul indicated in Galatians 4:19 "My little children, of whom I travail in birth again until Christ be formed in you."

Therefore, let us not let the difficulties we may encounter in our quest to imitate Christ discourage us. Instead, let us fix our minds on the ultimate goal, knowing that the reward and joy that await us far surpass any present hardships. With the mind of Christ guiding us, we can endure the process, overcome obstacles, and ultimately attain the fullness of perfection that God desires for us.

Chapter 11

Identifying with Christ's Sufferings

The Cross: Our salvation and model

Scripture provides us with the ultimate model and example in Jesus. We are called to look to Him and strive to imitate His character, teachings, and actions. Jesus exemplified selfless love, compassion, humility, forgiveness, and obedience to God's will. By studying His life and teachings, we gain insight into how to live a life that pleases God and blesses others.

Jesus, the Word made flesh, came to demonstrate the possibilities a human being can achieve when they experience the transformative power of Christ. He is our perfect model, but in order for us to imitate Him, we must begin on a level playing field.

The distinction between us and Jesus is that He was without sin, while we are sinners. Jesus went to the Cross for two primary reasons:

1. To save humanity from sin: By dying on the cross, Jesus paid the penalty for sin and demonstrated unconditional love for us all. Through faith, anyone who receives the gift of salvation is grafted into the family of God as a brother and enters into a level playing field with Jesus. Romans 8:29 states, "For whom

He foreknew, He also predestined to be conformed to the image of His Son, that He might be the firstborn among many brethren."

Jesus serves as the model, the firstborn of the spiritual family that conforms to the Image of God. In order to create many other models like Himself, He had to die. As stated in John 12:24, "I assure you and most solemnly say to you, unless a grain of wheat falls into the earth and dies, it remains alone [all in one, just one grain, never more]. But if it dies, it produces much grain and yields a harvest."

2. To show us the way to glorification through suffering: As written in 1 Peter 2:21, "For to this you have been called, because Christ also suffered for you, leaving you an example, so that you might follow in his steps." Jesus's death and suffering serve as examples for us to imitate, with the same principles leading to similar results. Some of the examples Jesus left us through sacrifice, suffering, and death are as follows:

Revelation 5:12 states, "Saying with a loud voice, Worthy is the Lamb that was slain to receive power, riches, wisdom, strength, honour, glory, and blessing." Jesus was slain (died) to receive all the rewards mentioned in the passage above. This shows us that through sacrifice, there is always a reward. No pain, no glory. No mess, no message.

In John 10:17, Jesus says, "Therefore My Father loves Me, because I lay down My life that I may take it again. No one takes it from Me, but I lay it down for Myself." Jesus showed us how He earned the Father's love through the sacrifice of humility, even obedience unto death.

***

The Humbled and Exalted Christ

In Philippians 2:5-7, we are encouraged to have the same mindset as Christ regarding suffering. It says, "Let this mind be in you, which was also in Christ Jesus, who, being in the form of God, did not consider it robbery to be equal with God, but made Himself of no reputation, taking the form of a bondservant and coming in the likeness of men." We see that Jesus, who was once in the form of God, humbled Himself by setting aside His divinity to qualify to die. He took on a different form as a bondservant in the likeness of men. This mindset was common to Jesus. He understood that through humility, one can be exalted in due time, as stated in 1 Peter 5:6, "Therefore humble yourselves under the mighty hand of God, that He may exalt you in due time."

When Jesus took on the form of a man, He once again humbled Himself, this time in obedience to death. As stated in Philippians 2:8, "And being found in appearance as a man, He humbled Himself and became obedient to the point of death, even the death of the cross."

The result of Jesus's humility, sacrifice, and death was exaltation. Philippians 2:9 says, "Therefore God also has highly exalted Him and given Him the name which is above every name, that at the name of Jesus every knee should bow, of those in heaven, and of those on earth, and of those under the earth, and that every tongue should confess that Jesus Christ is Lord, to the glory of God the Father."

It is important to remember that the scriptures above begin with the instruction to have the same mindset as Christ. In other words, what Jesus did was exemplary, and we are called to follow in His footsteps. Luke 9:23 says, "Then He said to them all, 'If anyone desires to come after Me, let him deny himself, and take up his cross daily, and follow Me.'"

Once we are enrolled in God's rehabilitation program through salvation, we are immediately seen and declared as brothers, with Jesus being the first among many. Just as Jesus went to the cross to receive rewards of a name above every other name, riches, and glory, and to be glorified, we too are called to participate in this process.

Chapter 12

Our Spirituality

The Journey from Babyhood to Spiritual Maturity

In addressing the believers in 1 Corinthians 3:1, Paul acknowledges that he could not speak to them as spiritual individuals but as carnal, as babies in Christ. This highlights the understanding that spirituality is a journey of growth and advancement, and the recipients of Paul's message were still in the early stages of their spiritual development. They resembled infants who had not yet reached maturity. A similar comparison can be found in Galatians 4:1, which states, "Now I say that the heir, as long as he is a child, differeth in nothing from a servant, though he be lord of all." During this phase, there are notable similarities between baby Christians and unbelievers.

However, it is important to note that believers in this babyhood stage are not meant to remain there indefinitely. They are encouraged to desire the nourishment and sustenance found in the milk of the Word so that they may grow and mature spiritually. It is common for baby Christians to exhibit behaviours similar to those of carnal men, influenced by their human nature and the limitations of their five senses. This is evident in 1 Corinthians 3:3, which states, "For ye are yet carnal; for whereas there is among you envying, strife, and divisions, are ye not carnal, and walk as men?" These manifestations of carnality can be attributed to a lack of growth or an inadequate understanding of how spiritual growth is meant to be attained.

***

The Relationship between the Spirit and the Flesh

In the journey of immersing oneself in the Word, one learns valuable lessons after spending quality time in the school of the Spirit, also known as the rehabilitation center. As one progresses, the topic of identity becomes significant—knowing who you truly are and then moving forward to understand what you possess, which is separate from your own being. For instance, your physical body is something you have, but it does not define your true self.

There are two aspects of growth: the growth of the spirit and the growth of the flesh, referring to the physical body. Both have the potential to develop, improve, and mature. However, the growth of the spirit does not commence until a significant event occurs. The journey towards spiritual growth does not begin with striving to grow spiritually; rather, it begins with being born again. Growth follows after being born again. Unfortunately, many individuals make the mistake of attempting to feed and nourish themselves spiritually before they have even experienced the new birth. They lack certainty about their spiritual rebirth. It is crucial to be certain of your spiritual birth before focusing on your growth. This is a common challenge among Christians. They desire to grow in the things of God before being certain of their spiritual rebirth. However, growth and maturity can only be realized after the birth of a child. Being certain of your spiritual rebirth is essential.

But what happens when you are born again is that a completely new Spirit enters an old body. To illustrate this, when you experience the new birth, it is like a fresh pilot stepping into a 150-year-old plane. The plane itself is old and worn out, but the pilot is supposed to bring a fresh perspective. Thus, the new pilot, who is young and full of vigor, must start making adjustments to the flaws of the old body. However, the ideal situation is for the old plane to make adjustments to accommodate the new pilot, which represents the renewal of the body.

Sometimes, when people encounter certain shortcomings, they begin to question if they are truly born again. The new spiritual man has entered the old vessel, but it is important to recognize that in modern vehicles, many individuals may struggle to figure out how to start an old car, let alone drive it. However, the owner-driver of that old vehicle, without much conscious effort, can start the car and drive away, even absentmindedly. In this scenario, it is evident that it is not the car that has adapted to the owner-driver, but rather the owner-driver who has made the necessary adjustments to operate a faulty vehicle. Similarly, many Christians find themselves continuously sinning and making mistakes. The new Spirit within them has made compromises to enable them to navigate their imperfect bodies. Consequently, the Spirit has become enslaved. It is no longer the body making adjustments to align with the demands of the Spirit; instead, the Spirit is adapting to the flaws of the physical body.

***

Understanding Spirituality and the Role of the Flesh

Growth is a multifaceted concept that includes both the development of the Spirit and the development of the flesh. When we talk about spirituality, we frequently associate it with the Spirit, referring to the nature of the Spirit within us. However, it is critical to understand that spirituality is primarily concerned with the state of the spirit itself.

Spirituality, in its true essence, is not limited to the realm of the Spirit alone. It is done and felt through our physical bodies, or flesh.

Similarly, a child cannot be labelled as "childish" because such behaviour is expected of them. Only when an adult exhibits immaturity is he or she considered childish. Similarly, a spirit cannot be labelled as spiritual because that is its expected nature. However, in order to achieve spirituality, something that is not inherently spiritual, such as the flesh, must be involved. Spirituality can be realised and attained by engaging and expressing spiritual attributes through the flesh.

It is a significant transformation when our physical bodies actively participate in spirituality. It means that our old vessel, our body, is adapting and aligning with the newly born spirit. This alignment allows for the harmonious union of our spiritual and physical selves, allowing us to fully embrace and live out spirituality.

The miraculous event of Jesus walking on water is an example of spirituality. The involvement of the flesh, the physical body, in carrying out the actions of the Spirit, rather than the Spirit alone, is responsible for the miracle in this extraordinary act. Can spirits, after all, not walk on water? Spirits are incapable of drowning in water. As a result, the genuine miracle lies in determining which aspect of Jesus is truly performing this remarkable deed. When the physical body performs actions that are normally attributed to the Spirit alone, this is spirituality manifested through the flesh. True spirituality is revealed in this demonstration.

It is critical to understand the distinction between the Spirit's mind and your own mind, as well as the relationship between the spirit and the body. You enter a state of harmony and maturity as you observe your physical body aligning itself with the principles and teachings of the Spirit rather than the Spirit conforming to accommodate the body. When the spirit constantly adapts to accommodate a flawed vessel, it indicates that the spirit is not finding fulfilment along its journey.

According to 1 Corinthians 2:16, we are reminded that no one can fully comprehend or instruct the Lord's mind. However, as Christians, we have the privilege of having Christ's mind. This mind of Christ is the same as the mind of the Spirit. As a result, we must strive to align our thoughts and behaviours with the teachings and divine guidance of the Spirit.

The fulfilment of the law's righteousness within us is confirmed in Romans 8:4: "So that the righteous requirement of the law might be fulfilled in us, who walk not according to the flesh but according to the Spirit." Our bodies conform to God's righteous standards when we walk in accordance with the Spirit. This alignment promotes maturity and spiritual development.

Furthermore, according to Romans 8:9, "but you are not in the flesh, but in the Spirit, if indeed the Spirit of God dwells in you." This verse emphasises that, as believers, we are no longer confined to the realm of the flesh alone but are also in the Spirit. The Holy Spirit resides within us, empowering us to live in accordance with the Spirit's guidance and promptings.

God's promise is revealed in Joel 2:28, which says, "And it shall come to pass afterward, that I will pour out my Spirit on all flesh; your sons and your daughters shall prophesy." This promise emphasises that the Holy Spirit will be poured out on all flesh, not just spirits. The goal of this outpouring is to empower the physical body to participate in spiritual activities such as prophecy. These spiritual acts are carried out through the use of the physical body as an instrument.

When the text mentions "your sons and daughters," it emphasises the participation of the flesh, represented by sons and daughters, in these spiritual activities. Because the Spirit transcends gender, he is not designated as a son or a daughter. There is no distinction between male and female in the realm of the Spirit. The key concept to grasp is that the flesh becomes the vessel through which spiritual acts, such as prophecy, are expressed when the Spirit is present.

God's purpose becomes clear when the Spirit is poured out on all flesh. He is bringing the Ark of the Covenant to completion within you. When you received the Holy Spirit, He came and established His dwelling place within you. In the Old Testament, the Holy Spirit would come upon individuals, but it wasn't until Pentecost that He began to dwell within them. As a result, the Holy Spirit now resides within you, transforming you into the Ark of the Covenant. Your physical body is comparable to acacia wood, but with the indwelling Holy Spirit, you now possess divine gold within. However, just as the ark of the covenant had gold on both the inside and outside, with acacia wood in between, God wants you to have the divine presence not only within your physical body but also radiating outward.

The divine nature should radiate beyond the confines of your physical body as the Holy Spirit overflows from within you. Anyone who comes into contact with you and touches your physical form will actually come into contact with the divine presence. It is a transformative journey of becoming fully immersed in God's nature, where your earthly flesh gradually fades away and becomes imperceptible. When others look at you, they see God's manifestation. No one will ever perceive your earthly nature again once the process of enveloping your flesh with divinity is complete. This is why God promises to pour out His Spirit on all flesh, allowing for profound transformation and divine overlaying.

***

Living by the Spoken Word and Cultivating Spiritual Growth

In Matthew 4:4, Jesus proclaimed that "man shall not live by bread alone but by every word that proceedeth out of the mouth of God." It prompts us to explore which man Jesus was referring to in this statement. Indeed, He was addressing the realm of the flesh. When Jesus mentioned that man cannot live by bread alone, He specifically alluded to the man who relies solely on physical bread for sustenance. It is important to note that this man cannot be the spirit because Jesus was specifically referring to physical bread in this particular text. The spiritual man, being connected to the divine, does not depend on or find nourishment in physical bread. The spirit man requires spiritual sustenance.

This aligns with the teachings of Deuteronomy 8:3, where it is written, "Man doth not live by bread alone, but by every word that proceedeth out of the mouth of the Lord." The emphasis here is on the fact that man's life is not solely sustained by physical food but also by the words spoken by God.

By highlighting that the physical man cannot live by bread alone, Jesus affirmed the significance of a deeper sustenance. The words "but by every word" in Matthew 4:4 reiterate the importance of the spoken word in the life of the physical man. It implies that the physical man should reach a point where he understands how to live by the power of God's spoken word while still being in the physical realm.

Jesus did not instruct us, as physical beings, to completely abstain from eating bread. However, He emphasised that bread alone could not sustain us. Therefore, after nourishing our physical bodies with breakfast, we must also seek sustenance from the spoken word of God. It is through the word that proceeds out of the mouth of God that our flesh finds true life and vitality. Without the word, the flesh is in a state of decay or even spiritual death.

It is crucial to distinguish between the written word of God and the word that proceeds out of His mouth. The Scriptures, which were captured in the pages of the Bible by men inspired by the Holy Spirit, constitute the written word of God. However, there is also the ongoing, present, continuous word of God that proceeds from His mouth—the spoken word. While reading the written word, there may come a moment when we encounter the spoken word. As we read the written word of God, we must be attentive to the spoken word as well. We should seek to understand what God is currently saying through the words we are reading.

An excellent example of this is found in the story of the Ethiopian Eunuch, who was reading from the book of Isaiah. In that instance, Philip approached him and asked if he understood what he was reading. Philip recognized that comprehension comes not only from reading the written word but also from hearing the spoken word. The Ethiopian Eunuch acknowledged his need for guidance, stating, "How can I understand, except some man should guide me?" This account illustrates that the written scriptures alone cannot grant understanding; we must engage in both reading and hearing.

The Scripture in 2 Corinthians 3:6 further affirms this truth, declaring that "the letter killeth, but the spirit giveth life." This passage highlights the distinction between mere intellectual knowledge of the written word and the life-giving power found in the revelation of the Holy Spirit. It is through hearing the spoken word and being led by the Spirit that we truly come to life and gain understanding.

The practice of spirituality in the flesh is facilitated in the following manner: While physically reading the Bible, there should be a spiritual engagement by the flesh—a yearning to hear what God, who is spirit, is communicating. The words that proceed from the mouth of God, spoken through the Holy Spirit, are what the flesh lives by. This is the very reason why Jesus, who is the Word, came as a life-giving spirit (1 Corinthians 15:45). He bestowed upon us the same spirit before His ascension so that He might dwell within us and reveal the Word, which is the bread of life, enabling us to live according to it.

The scriptural reference in Romans 8:11 supports this truth: "And if the Spirit of Him who raised Jesus from the dead lives in you, He who raised Christ Jesus from the dead will also give life to your mortal bodies through His Spirit, who lives in you." It emphasizes that the Spirit of God, residing within us, not only raised Jesus from the dead but also imparted life to our mortal bodies. It is through His Spirit, dwelling in us, that we receive the divine life.

Therefore, the message remains consistent: When we engage in the physical act of reading the Bible, we must also cultivate a spiritual practice of actively desiring to hear God's voice. This is accomplished through the Holy Spirit, who dwells within us and imparts life. By yielding to the Spirit's leading and receiving the revelation of the Word, which is the bread of life, we experience the transformative power of spirituality in our fleshly existence.

When encountering a scripture like Deuteronomy 28:13 that states, "And the Lord shall make thee the head, and not the tail," it is essential to personalize it while also considering its contextual meaning. To fully grasp its significance, we must understand to whom the letter was written and about whom it was referring. While desiring the words to apply to ourselves, there must be a confirmation, a spoken word that affirms our inclusion in the written word, and we shall live by it.

Once the confirmation is received, understanding begins to unfold. For example, when God declares that we are the head and not the tail, we must explore the roles of the head and the tail. God will provide us with insight and revelation. It may be that while we strive to become the head, the original recipient of the word was not in that position at the time it was written. However, for us, we are currently the head, and we need to recognize this truth. We may question why there is no visible evidence of our headship. In such cases, we embark on a further investigation through engagement with the word.

We inquire about what it means to show that we are the head. Whose acknowledgment are we seeking? If God has already made us the head, what serves as proof or evidence of our headship? We delve into our understanding of the concept of being the head. It is important to note that we should not strive in prayer to become the head when, in reality, we are already the head. Our prayer should focus on making the head aware of its true identity.

Many of the things we seek as Christians remain elusive, not because we haven't found them but because we lack awareness of their reality due to a lack of understanding. Therefore, our pursuit should be rooted in gaining understanding and making ourselves aware of the truths and realities that God has already established for us.

Many Christians express frustration when they don't see their prayers answered or witness the fulfillment of God's promises in His word. However, the issue lies not in acquiring what we desire but rather in how we cultivate and nurture what we already have. Once we are born again, our focus shifts to maturing our spirit rather than seeking rebirth. We acknowledge that the Bible serves as spiritual food, but as we progress, the Word becomes nourishment for our flesh as well. The man who cannot live by bread alone begins to live by every word that proceeds from God's mouth. This man refers to the flesh, which must continually seek knowledge and understanding while being aware of the Holy Spirit's presence.

We emphasize the need to be more conscious of the Holy Spirit than of the flesh because, as we strive for maturity, we embark on a journey of self-disappearance. It is no longer about us living, but allowing Him to live through us. While a part of the flesh remains, we are being transformed into the image of God, becoming who He is. Eventually, we reach a point where the flesh is no longer in control and we are influenced and led by the Holy Spirit. This signifies the attainment of sonship, or maturity. The flesh now follows the Spirit, and the physical manifestations of the flesh align with the spirit. The spirituality of the flesh is perfected, as everything the flesh does reflects the workings of the Spirit.

To make the Word our lifestyle, we must begin by ceasing to struggle with our flesh. Our flesh itself is not the enemy; rather, it is carnality that opposes us. We should recognize our flesh as a gift from God, and when we view it as such, we will no longer struggle with what God has bestowed upon us as an advantage.

Therefore, in order to practice spirituality, the flesh must emulate the behavior of a spirit.

Before making any decisions, we should allow our flesh to consult and seek guidance from the Spirit. If the Spirit advises against a particular course of action and the flesh obediently refrains, it becomes a spiritual practice exhibited by the flesh. The spirituality of the flesh is evident when it ceases to act according to its own desires and only carries out what the Spirit would do. When the flesh is willing to receive instructions from the Spirit, it signifies a level of maturity.

It is crucial to have understanding so that we do not strive to become what we already are. We must remember that it was due to a lack of understanding that the devil took advantage of Adam and Eve, deceiving them into thinking that they would be like God if they ate the forbidden fruit when, in fact, they were already like God. Lack of understanding can lead to the manipulation of the Word, which is inherently good, and result in spiritual death.

In the Bible, there are events and circumstances that we would not desire to happen to us. There are dreadful occurrences, and, to be honest, we do not want everything written in the Bible to manifest in our lives. Therefore, we should not simply raise our Bibles and declare that every aspect of it should happen to us. Instead, we must carefully select and pursue what aligns with our desires. The Bible contains stories of individuals who committed suicide, thieves who insulted God, wise people, cursed individuals, and fools. Hence, we should seek after what we desire and discern the voice that asks us, "Do you understand what you are reading?" Our response should acknowledge the need for interpretation and understanding. Just as Philip assisted the Ethiopian Eunuch in comprehending the scriptures, we too may require guidance and explanations.

The Ethiopian Eunuch may have attempted to follow the advice of someone who encouraged him to read his Bible diligently (which is indeed good advice). He chose to study the Scriptures at home, thinking that he did not need to assemble with other believers in church. However, the Holy Spirit orchestrated the encounter with Philip to demonstrate that the Eunuch lacked an understanding of the principles of comprehension. This serves as a reminder that simply reading the scriptures without proper guidance does not grant access to understanding. Therefore, if we encounter someone in a similar situation, we must show them the importance of seeking interpretation and avoid falling into confusion.

In our pursuit of understanding the Scriptures, it is essential to have an interpreter. The Holy Spirit is the interpreter of the written word, and He works in conjunction with our yielded souls to bring illumination. However, the ministry of men is not to be disregarded. Men are an important medium through which the Holy Spirit imparts His influence and enlightenment in the body of Christ. We cannot attain perfection or deep understanding by isolating ourselves and disregarding the role of men. Such an attitude stems from pride, and God opposes the proud but gives grace to the humble. Even the Holy Spirit Himself works through men. Throughout the Bible, we see God seeking individuals, asking, "Who shall go for us?" In the New Testament, the Holy Spirit declares that our bodies have been purchased at a price and that we are not our own. Men serve as vessels through which the Holy Spirit operates. This is why it is the Spirit and the bride (the body of Christ) that invite others to come.

In 1 Corinthians 12:4–12, the Holy Spirit distributes gifts to every believer so that the manifestation of the Spirit is not confined to one person but may benefit all. As members of one body, we are expected to bring what we have received from the Holy Spirit to the table, allowing everyone to benefit from it. This fosters unity, oneness, and completeness. For this purpose, Christ has given us men in the body of Christ, including apostles, prophets, evangelists, pastors, and teachers. Their role is to perfect the saints, carry out the work of the ministry, and edify the body of Christ, as stated in Ephesians 4:11–12.

We are admonished not to forsake the assembly of believers because it is in that gathering that we bring together all the gifts that the Holy Spirit has bestowed upon each individual. It is in this context that we find understanding and experience the sharpening of one another, just as iron sharpens iron. No one is an island in the body of Christ; we are all members who cannot do without one another. Therefore, forsaking the gathering of believers and seeking to find and understand God in isolation is false and a deceptive scheme of the enemy. The enemy desires to isolate the brethren so that he can attack and consume them, just like a lion isolates its prey from the pack. Embracing this lie puts us at risk of falling away from the faith or experiencing stunted growth. We must reject this deception and recognize the vital importance of fellowship and unity within the body of Christ.

***

Must Worship God in Spirit and in Truth

Many people engage in worshipping God with their spirits, but they often fall short in understanding and implementing the truth component of worship. According to the teachings of the Bible, truth is not limited to factual accuracy; it encompasses a deeper spiritual understanding, a relationship with God, and moral integrity.

Here are several key aspects of truth as revealed in Scripture:

1. Truth as an Attribute of God: The Bible affirms that God Himself is the ultimate source of truth. Jesus declares in John 14:6 that He is "the way, the truth, and the life."

2. Truth as Spiritual Enlightenment: Jesus proclaims in John 8:32 that knowing the truth sets people free. This implies that understanding and embracing the truth, particularly the truth found in God and His Word, liberates us from ignorance, bondage, and falsehood.

3. Truth in Relationship with Christ: Truth is intricately linked to a personal relationship with Jesus Christ. John 1:14 describes Jesus as "full of grace and truth." Following Christ involves accepting His teachings, submitting to His lordship, and experiencing the transformative power of His truth.

4. Truthfulness and Honesty: The Bible consistently emphasises the virtues of truthfulness and honesty. Proverbs 12:22 states that "the Lord detests lying lips, but he delights in people who are trustworthy."

5. Truth as a Moral Standard: Truth serves as a moral benchmark against which human actions and behaviours are evaluated. Ephesians 4:25 exhorts believers to speak truthfully and avoid falsehood and deception.

By understanding these dimensions of truth and integrating them into our worship, we can approach God with a more complete and sincere devotion, aligning our spirits, minds, and actions with the truth He has revealed.

Aspects 1 to 3 in the list above highlight the description and identity of truth, while aspects 4 and 5 emphasise the practical application of truth. Worship is an active practise that involves reverential and devoted acts or expressions directed towards a deity, higher power, or spiritual entity. Therefore, when Jesus instructed us on how to worship God, I believe He was providing guidance on the act of worship, as stated in John 4:24: "God is spirit, and his worshippers must worship in the Spirit and in truth."

The act of worshipping God in the Spirit necessitates our submission and openness to the influence of the Holy Spirit, allowing Him to shape and guide our worship directed towards God. The Holy Spirit has a profound understanding of the deep things of God, comprehending the mind of God and how He desires to be worshipped. Through our willingness to be led by the Holy Spirit, we offer God the worship that is truly deserving, in a precise manner that aligns with His desires.

According to Jesus' instruction, worshipping God encompasses two essential facets. However, while many are familiar with the first facet of worshipping in Spirit, the second facet of worshipping in truth appears to be misunderstood, misinterpreted, or overlooked. It seems as though there is a tendency to believe that once we fulfil the spiritual dimension, the aspect of truth is automatically satisfied. Unfortunately, this assumption is incorrect.

Truth in the context of worship can be likened to a coin with two sides. A coin is traditionally recognised to have an obverse (head) side and a reverse (tail) side, each displaying distinct designs. This dual-sided nature is crucial for identification, authentication, and standardisation of currency. Similarly, truth encompasses two essential aspects.

In worship, truth requires the engagement of both sides. One side of truth is love, which represents the expression of genuine affection, devotion, and compassion towards God. The other side is hate, which signifies the rejection of falsehood, sin, and anything that opposes God's truth. Both sides are integral to true worship.

Just as a coin cannot be complete without both sides, true worship necessitates the acknowledgment and incorporation of love and hate within the truth. Neglecting either side diminishes the authenticity and depth of worship. A coin cannot be recognised as valid currency if it has two heads or two tails; they must be opposites. Similarly, in the practise of worshipping in truth, both aspects of the truth coin must be fully embraced. On one side, there should be love, and on the other side, there should be hatred. Love and love, or hate and hate, undermine the essence of true worship in relation to truth.

Amos 5:15 reminds us to "Hate evil and love good." When it comes to worshipping God in truth, it is not enough to only love God and all that is good with our whole heart, as this one-sided approach negates the implementation of truth. Alongside our love for God, righteousness, and all that is good, we must also harbour a godly displeasure and hatred towards evil and anything that does not glorify God. It is the harmonious combination of these two aspects of truth that perfects the act of worshipping God in truth.

Paul, speaking about Love in Action, emphasises in Romans 12:9 that love must be sincere. To be sincere in our love, we must genuinely hate what is evil and cling to what is good. A love that only embraces what is good without an equally strong aversion to evil is insincere and incomplete.

In present times, it is noticeable that many Christians demonstrate a profound love for God, but at the same time, they harbour affection for evil. They faithfully attend church and engage in worship, yet they also partake in activities that promote ungodliness and immorality, such as visiting nightclubs or engaging in boozy gatherings. James 3:9–10 addresses this issue, stating, "With the tongue we praise our Lord and Father, and with it we curse human beings, who have been made in God's likeness. Out of the same mouth come praise and cursing. My brothers and sisters, this should not be."

This passage exposes the prevalent state of many Christians who have failed to grasp the concept of loving good and hating evil. Their lack of understanding places them in compromising situations where their unrestrained inclination towards evil compromises their devotion to God. Although they genuinely love God, they are prone to engaging in sinful acts when faced with temptation. To overcome this predicament, it is essential to consciously embrace love for what is good and cultivate a genuine hatred towards evil.

By intentionally choosing to love good and hate evil, we create a framework that enables us to embrace righteousness and reject ungodliness. This conscious act of love and hate fosters a sincere and unadulterated worship of the truth. It serves as a safeguard against compromising our devotion to God and ensures that our worship remains genuine, wholehearted, and untainted by the influences of evil.

The essence of God's nature is revealed in Proverbs 12:22, which declares, "The Lord detests lying lips, but he delights in people who are trustworthy." This verse illustrates God's love for what is good and His hatred for evil. Likewise, Ephesians 4:25 exhorts us to put away lying and speak truthfully to one another, emphasising the importance of honesty and truth in our interactions as members of one body.

To express and implement the truth sincerely, it is essential to combine love and hate. One cannot claim to love God while also harbouring a love for the devil. Similarly, one cannot exhibit an act of truth by hating both good and evil. As Matthew 6:24 states, it is impossible to serve two masters simultaneously. "For either you will hate the one and love the other; or else you will hold to the one and despise the other. You cannot serve God and mammon."

The truth is the transformative force that sanctifies Christians, setting them apart from the evil and corruption prevalent in the world. In 2 Corinthians 6:14–16, believers are cautioned against being unequally yoked with unbelievers and forming alliances that contradict their faith. Righteousness cannot be partnered with lawlessness, light cannot have fellowship with darkness, and there is no harmony between Christ and Satan. As the temple of the living God, we are instructed to separate ourselves from unbelievers and refrain from touching what is unclean, and God promises to graciously receive and welcome us.

However, it is important to note that God does not remove us from the corrupt system of the world, as Jesus expressed in John 17:15 when he prayed that believers would not be taken out of the world. Instead, sanctification occurs through the process of truth. In the later part of John 17:15–17, Jesus prayed for believers to be kept from evil, highlighting their distinction from the world. Sanctification takes place through the truth, which is God's Word.

To summarise, truth encompasses a love for what is good and a hatred for evil. The process of sanctification involves God separating us from ourselves by directing our affections towards Him and safeguarding our hearts from the allure of evil. Through this process of truth, we are consecrated and dedicated to God.

Jesus, who is identified as the truth and the Word, wields a two-edged sword according to the Scriptures. This sword serves both offensive and defensive purposes. Offensively, the Word of God can dismantle falsehood, refute false teachings, and proclaim the truth of the gospel. Defensively, it empowers believers to stand firm against the schemes of the enemy, safeguarding their faith. Walking in truth entails aligning one's life with God's commands and His revealed will, demonstrating a love for what is good and a hatred for what is evil. Psalm 97:10 instructs those who love the Lord to hate evil. The order of love and hate in the implementation of truth is crucial. It is imperative to love what is good and hate what is evil. If we invert this order, calling good evil and evil good, the Bible warns of impending woe. Isaiah 5:20 states, "Woe to those who call evil good, and good evil; Who put darkness for light, and light for darkness; Who put bitter for sweet, and sweet for bitter!"

***

Abstinence from Alcohol: Making Room for the Holy Spirit's Intoxication

In a world where alcohol is often seen as a means of celebration and relaxation, there is a powerful concept that encourages us to embrace a different kind of intoxication. Abstinence from alcohol can be viewed as an act of self-denial that allows us to make room for the Holy Spirit to intoxicate us. By examining the effects of alcohol on our faculties and comparing them to the transformative power of the Holy Spirit, we can better understand why the Bible admonishes us to be filled with the Spirit rather than drunk with wine.

Alcohol's Intoxication: Alcohol, when consumed, has a profound effect on our mental, emotional, and physical faculties. It impairs our judgement, distorts our perception, and can lead to bold and influential behaviour. We often refer to this state as being "drunk." It is a condition where our senses are dulled, our inhibitions are lowered, and our ability to make sound decisions is compromised.

When under the influence of alcohol, our intellect is impaired. We struggle to think clearly; our cognitive abilities are diminished, and our judgement becomes clouded. Our emotions, too, are affected, as alcohol can swing us between extreme highs and lows. Our behaviour may become erratic, and our actions may lack rationality or self-control. In essence, alcohol's intoxication alters our state of being and inhibits our ability to function optimally.

Biblical Guidance and the Holy Spirit: The Bible offers guidance on the consumption of alcohol, cautioning against the perils of excessive indulgence. In Ephesians 5:18, the apostle Paul writes, "And do not get drunk with wine, for that is debauchery, but be filled with the Spirit." This verse emphasises the need to be filled with the Holy Spirit rather than intoxicated with wine. It presents an alternative form of intoxication, one that is transformative and aligns us with God's will.

The Intoxication of the Holy Spirit: When we allow the Holy Spirit to fill our souls, it brings about a spiritual intoxication that far surpasses the effects of alcohol. This divine intoxication does not impair our faculties but instead enhances and uplifts them. The Holy Spirit enlightens our intellect, granting us wisdom and understanding. It sharpens our discernment, enabling us to make sound decisions and navigate life's challenges with clarity.

Similarly, the Holy Spirit influences our emotions, filling our hearts with joy, peace, love, and other fruits of the Spirit. This intoxication doesn't lead to unpredictable swings or erratic behaviour; rather, it brings about emotional stability and spiritual maturity. It aligns our desires with God's desires and transforms our character.

The Soul as a Cup: To better understand the concept of making room for the Holy Spirit, we can liken our soul to a cup. Just as a cup can be filled with different substances, our soul can be filled either with the intoxicating effects of alcohol or with the transformative power of the Holy Spirit. When we indulge in alcohol, our cup is filled with a temporary and fleeting satisfaction. However, when we choose abstinence, we empty our cup of alcohol's influence, creating space for the Holy Spirit to overflow and saturate our being.

***

Living a Supernatural Life: Understanding the Difference between the Supernatural and the Spectacular

As believers, we are called to live a spiritual life characterised by the supernatural influence of the Holy Spirit. It is crucial, however, to discern the distinction between the supernatural and the spectacular. Looking at the life of Jesus, who exemplified a spiritual life filled with the Holy Spirit, we can gain insight into this difference and the importance of not pursuing the spectacular as the norm.

1. Jesus: Living a Spirit-Filled Life Jesus Christ, the Son of God, lived a life completely surrendered to the Holy Spirit. From His conception to His resurrection, Jesus' every moment was characterised by the supernatural influence of the Holy Spirit. He performed miracles, healed, and taught with authority, all by the power of the Spirit. His life serves as an example for us, illustrating the transformative impact of a spiritual life led by the Holy Spirit.

2. The Supernatural and the Spectacular: It is crucial to differentiate between the supernatural and the spectacular in our understanding of living a spiritual life. The supernatural encompasses the constant presence and guidance of the Holy Spirit, empowering us to live according to God's will. It includes acts

of obedience, love, and service, guided by the Spirit, as a part of our daily lives. On the other hand, the spectacular refers to extraordinary displays of power or miracles that occur infrequently and are not the norm in our spiritual journey.

3. Jesus' Temptation: The Choice to Prioritise the Supernatural An illustration of the distinction between the supernatural and the spectacular can be found in Jesus' temptation in the wilderness. When tempted by Satan to turn stones into bread or to jump off a cliff, Jesus chose not to pursue the spectacular. He understood that a life solely focused on the spectacular would deviate from the supernatural essence of His mission.

4. The Primacy of the Supernatural in Jesus' Ministry: Jesus' ministry was predominantly characterised by the supernatural, not the spectacular. He regularly healed the sick, cast out demons, and taught with authority, all as a manifestation of the ongoing influence of the Holy Spirit. These acts showcased God's love and power in everyday situations, demonstrating the supernatural aspect of His ministry.

5. The Occasional Spectacular: While Jesus did perform some spectacular miracles, such as walking on water or multiplying bread, these acts were not the norm in His ministry. They occurred on specific occasions and served distinct purposes. Jesus prioritised the supernatural—the constant flow of the Holy Spirit's guidance and power—over the pursuit of the spectacular.

6. Embracing the supernatural and exercising discernment: As believers, our focus should be on cultivating a deep relationship with God and allowing the supernatural influence of the Holy Spirit to transform us from within. While miracles and extraordinary acts can occur, they should not be our primary pursuit or expectation. Instead, our emphasis should be on daily obedience, love, and service, reflecting the supernatural aspect of our spiritual journey.

Chapter 13

Our Active Engagement in the Growth Process

Yielding our will to the process of suffering

Due to the alternative system created by the fall of man, humanity, which possesses free will, now has a choice to make between the flesh and the Spirit. But man is expected to exercise his free will in submission to the Spirit of God. This submission allows for the establishment of a partnership where God can work through man. However, in the midst of inhabiting this corrupt body, man must learn how to exert control over it and make the choice to yield to the Spirit.

The daily crucifixion of the corrupt body is necessary because it stands in opposition to God's will. This is also the reason why the body needs to be transformed before entering heaven. In 1 Corinthians 15:50, it is stated, "Now this I say, brethren, that flesh and blood cannot inherit the kingdom of God; neither doth corruption inherit incorruption."

Even while Jesus was in the flesh before His death, He exemplified yielding His will to that of the Father. In Matthew 26:39, Jesus said, "My Father, if it is possible, may this cup be taken from me. Yet not as I will, but as you will."

He exercised His free will by willingly submitting to the process of growth and glorification. In John 10:16–17, He declared, "Therefore doth my Father love me, because I laid down my life, that I might take it again. No man takes it from me, but I lay it down for myself. I have power to lay it down, and I have power to take it again."

These examples from Jesus' life emphasise the importance of actively choosing to align our will with God's will. It is through the exercise of our free will in submission to God's Spirit that we experience growth, transformation, and ultimately, the glorification of our beings.

Jesus exemplified the principle that sacrifice is a prerequisite for growth and glorification. He willingly yielded Himself to the process, leaving us an example to follow. In Luke 9:23, Jesus said, "If any man will come after me, let him deny himself, take up his cross daily, and follow me."

Through Jesus's death, He paid the penalty for our sins, granting us access to the kingdom of God. This can be illustrated by the story of Takwana, a drug addict who, through the payment made by a counselor, is freed from the legal consequences of her actions and granted access to a rehabilitation center. However, once she is in the rehabilitation centre, she must actively participate in the process of breaking free from the control of the substance. Otherwise, her efforts to become clean would be in vain. Similarly, now that we are in the kingdom of God, we need to actively engage in the process that leads to our growth and glorification.

This process is often accompanied by suffering. Through the price Jesus paid, we are now in the kingdom, and God, who calls things into existence that do not yet exist, immediately grants us the position of heirs with Christ Jesus. However, just as Jesus laid down His life through many sufferings and was glorified, we need to follow His example to attain the level of glorification we desire. Romans 8:17 tells us that "we are heirs of God and joint-heirs with Christ if we suffer with Him, so that we may also be glorified together."

As children of God, redeemed by the blood of Jesus, we have been given the privilege of being heirs and joint-heirs with Christ. However, this privilege comes with the condition that we are willing to endure and embrace the process of suffering for His sake. Through this process, we align ourselves with the path Jesus walked, ultimately leading to our growth and participation in His glory.

Many Christians rejoice in being children of God but fail to grasp the significance of suffering for the purpose of growth and glorification. It is crucial to understand that not all forms of suffering lead to glorification. In fact, the Scripture warns us in 1 Peter 4:15, "But let none of you suffer as a murderer, or as a thief, or as an evildoer, or as a busybody in other men's matters."

Paul describes the type of suffering we are called to in 2 Timothy 2:8–13. He speaks of suffering for the sake of the gospel and enduring all things for the sake of the brethren. Similarly, we are urged to deny ourselves and follow Jesus. Any act of self-denial, endurance, or sacrifice we undertake for the sake of the kingdom is the kind of suffering that leads to glorification. For instance, to experience spiritual renewal and strength, it is not readily available through mere access to the kingdom. We must pay the price of suffering, which includes waiting upon the Lord, as stated in Isaiah 40:31, "But they that wait upon the Lord shall renew their strength." This provision is not freely accessible without paying the price of waiting. Therefore, it emphasises that only those who wait will experience the promised strength. In fact, the Scriptures inform us that it is possible to be depleted of strength, as Proverbs 24:10 states, "If thou faint in the day of adversity, thy strength is small."

Numerous examples in Scripture demonstrate the significance of suffering. Another notable illustration is found in the parable of the ten virgins. Five were wise, and five were foolish. We witness the foolish ones suffering the consequences of missing the bridegroom simply because they were not diligent enough to pay the price of suffering by having enough oil in their lamps. "If we suffer, we shall also reign with him; if we deny him, he also will deny us" (2 Timothy 2:12).

Self-denial and humility were central to the mindset of Christ, and we are encouraged to follow His example. The Scripture instructs us, "Let this mind be in you, which was also in Christ Jesus." It is necessary for us to crucify the flesh daily, putting our corrupt body under subjection, so that we may actively live out the life of Christ. As stated in Galatians 5:24, "And those who are Christ's have crucified the flesh with its passions and desires."

In Galatians 4:1-2, we are reminded that even though we are heirs with Christ, as long as we are still children, we do not differ from servants. This highlights the importance of growth. Once we mature and reach full stature, we can assume our position as lords over all.

The process of growth is described as being under tutors and governors for the purpose of learning. Through the washing of water by the Word, guided by these tutors, we are enabled to attain maturity, sonship, and perfection.

***

Tutors

Jesus, in Matthew 5:48, exhorted us to be perfect as our heavenly Father is perfect, emphasising that perfection is a requirement in the kingdom. While we can come to God just as we are, we are not meant to remain in a state of immaturity.

To achieve perfection, once we are enrolled in the kingdom, God places us under tutors who work towards our perfection, maturity, and sonship in Christ. This is described in Ephesians 4:11–15, where apostles, prophets, evangelists, pastors, and teachers are given for the purpose of perfecting the saints, equipping them for ministry, and building up the body of Christ. The goal is for all believers to come into unity of faith and knowledge of the Son of God, reaching a state of maturity and measuring up to the fullness of Christ. This maturity enables us to no longer be swayed by false doctrines or deceived by cunning men. Instead, we grow in truth and love, becoming fully aligned with Christ, who is the head.

As we listen to the words of our tutors, our faith is built, as Jesus explained in Romans 10:17, "So then faith comes by hearing, and hearing by the word of God." It is our responsibility to actively engage and cooperate with our tutors, paying attention to the Word of God. By doing so, we grow in faith, transitioning from milk to solid food, as described in Hebrews 5:14.

***

Faith

As we actively engage with the word of God spoken through our tutors, our faith is built, and it is crucial for us to exercise that faith. Without faith, it is impossible to please God, as stated in Hebrews 11:6.

Even if our faith is as small as a mustard seed, the Bible tells us that it is powerful enough to move mountains. However, we must guard against doubt and unbelief, as they hinder the effectiveness of the word. James 1:7-8 warns us that a person who doubts should not expect to receive anything from the Lord, and a double-minded individual is unstable in all their ways.

Whenever the word of God is spoken, it must be mixed with faith in order to benefit the hearer. Hebrews 4:2 states that the gospel was preached to both us and those in the past, but it did not profit them because they did not mix it with faith.

Therefore, it is our responsibility, as we receive instruction in the word, to combine it with faith for our spiritual growth and progress.

***

Confession

Even though we receive the word from our tutors and mix it with faith, it is essential to understand the power of confession, speaking out the words we have heard because a closed mouth can hinder our destiny.

As spiritual beings, no longer governed by the flesh or our natural selves, our soul and body are meant to be under the authority of our spirit. The Spirit within us is a life-giving Spirit, and therefore our words and confessions should be filled with the Spirit and life. Jesus emphasised this truth in John 6:63, saying, "It is the Spirit who gives life; the flesh profits nothing. The words that I speak to you are spirit, and they are life."

Confession played a significant role in our salvation, as Romans 10:10 states, "For with the heart one believes unto righteousness, and with the mouth confession is made unto salvation." Likewise, confession is vital in our journey towards sonship and maturity. We need to confess the word, declaring truths such as "I am the righteousness of God in Christ Jesus."

However, we must be mindful of the words we speak, for Proverbs 18:21 reminds us, "Death and life are in the power of the tongue, and those who love it will eat its fruit."

The power of death and life is activated through the tongue. This highlights the potency of words. Jesus himself is the Word, and through him, the world was created.

Even death has a process of manifestation, as seen in Romans 7:5, which speaks of how the motions of sin in our flesh bring forth fruit unto death. James 1:15 further explains that when lust is conceived, it gives birth to sin, and sin, when it is fully grown, brings forth death.

Speaking is a matter of choice, and God encourages us to choose life so that we may live. This highlights the importance of engaging our consciousness and being mindful of our words, as they have the power to activate either life or death.

As stated in Ephesians 4:29, we are urged not to let corrupt communication come out of our mouths but to speak what is good for edification, that it may impart grace to the hearers.

Perfection is achieved when our words are free from offence, without any distortion or perversion. Proverbs 15:4 teaches us that a wholesome tongue is a tree of life, but perverseness in speech is like a breach in the spirit. Our spirit, which is meant to govern our soul and body, sustains us when it is not wounded. Proverbs 18:14 reveals, "The spirit of a man will sustain his infirmity, but who can bear a broken spirit?" When our spirit is wounded, it becomes detrimental to our well-being. Perverse words have the potential to breach and wound the spirit, whereas wholesome words become a source of life.

James 3:1–13 describes the tongue as a fire that can defile the entire body. While it acknowledges that no human can tame the tongue, it does not imply that the spirit can. James even rebukes those who use their tongue to curse and bless, stating that it should not be so. This suggests that the tongue can indeed be tamed, but not by human effort alone. Thankfully, as Christians, we have the Holy Spirit to help us tame and direct our speech towards the path of life. According to James 3:2, if we can refrain from offending with our words, we have the ability to achieve perfection and gain control over our entire body. This becomes possible through the guidance of the Holy Spirit and by being selective in our choice of words, enabling us to attain maturity and bring our whole being into alignment with life.

Jesus also emphasised the importance of communication. In Luke 18:1, Jesus taught that men ought to pray continually and not faint. This means we should focus on prayer, which involves communicating with God through the Spirit. If we neglect prayer and fail to make confessions, we are essentially fainting. However, attaining maturity is impossible when we are in a state of fainting. If we find ourselves fainting in the face of adversity, it is an indication that our spiritual strength is lacking. We have yet to reach maturity or sonship in terms of strength.

Prayer was not originally part of man's original design. In the beginning, God communed directly with man. However, after the fall, prayer became the means through which communication with God was restored. Through prayer, we invite God into our lives and take on the responsibility of engaging with Him. For a natural man, prayer can be laborious and challenging. However, the Holy Spirit has been given to assist us in our weaknesses, praying through us and on our behalf. The sacrifice required is to wait on the Lord to renew our strength, drawing life and vitality from the Spirit to enable us to call upon God (Psalm 80:18).

We must be mindful of our confessions, as Isaiah 33:24 instructs us not to declare sickness. Instead, the people dwelling in God's presence shall have forgiveness of iniquity.

In the last days, there will be mockers who walk in ungodliness. These individuals separate themselves and lack the Spirit. However, as beloved children of God, we are called to build ourselves up on our most holy faith, praying in the

Holy Spirit (Jude 1:18–20). It is through praying in the Holy Spirit that we are strengthened and progress towards maturity, sonship, and perfection.

We must always remember that every word spoken will be accounted for. According to Matthew 12:36–37, every idle word will be judged. Our words have the power to justify or condemn us. Therefore, we must be cautious and intentional with our speech.

***

Overcoming the Test

Temptation: A test to embrace for advancement

Imagine a mountaineer standing at the base of a towering peak, gazing up at its majestic summit. He knows that reaching the top will require strength, endurance, and resilience. As he begins his ascent, he encounters various obstacles and challenges along the way, including treacherous terrain, unpredictable weather, and sheer cliffs. These obstacles, although daunting, serve as tests that push him to his limits.

In the same way, temptation can be seen as a test in our journey of faith. Just as the mountaineer faces obstacles, we encounter temptations that entice us to deviate from the path of righteousness. However, the Scriptures teach us that we should not be discouraged or seek to avoid temptations altogether. Instead, we are encouraged to embrace them with joy and a firm resolve.

James 1:2-4 (KJV) reminds us of this truth: "My brethren, count it all joy when ye fall into divers temptations, knowing this, that the trying of your faith worketh patience. But let patience have her perfect work, that you may be perfect and entire, wanting nothing."

Temptations, like tests, are designed to refine and strengthen our character. They challenge us to exercise our faith and develop spiritual maturity. Just as a mountaineer becomes stronger and more skilled as he conquers each obstacle, we too can grow in faith and character as we overcome temptations.

Rather than praying for temptations to be removed from our lives, our prayer should be for the grace and strength to overcome them. We should seek God's guidance and wisdom to navigate through the trials, knowing that they are part of our growth process. Just as the mountaineer relies on his training and equipment, we rely on God's Word, the Holy Spirit, and the support of fellow believers to help us overcome temptations.

When we embrace temptations as tests that refine us, our faith is strengthened, and we develop patience, perseverance, and resilience. As we allow patience to do its perfect work in us, we become more complete and lacking in nothing. Just as the mountaineer reaches the summit and experiences the fulfilment of his journey, we can attain spiritual maturity and experience the fullness of God's blessings when we overcome temptations with His grace.

Temptations: A test, not from God

Imagine a skilled and respected teacher who wants to assess the abilities of his students. He decides to conduct a series of tests to evaluate their knowledge and skills. However, he wants to make it clear that he is not responsible for creating the challenges they will face. He sets up the tests, but he does not manipulate the outcome or intentionally make the tasks difficult.

Similarly, in the realm of spiritual testing and temptation, James 1:13 reminds us: "Let no man say when he is tempted, I am tempted of God; for God cannot be tempted with evil, nor tempteth he any man." God, being holy and perfect, does not tempt us or lead us into sin. Just as the teacher in our illustration does not create difficulties for his students, God does not orchestrate temptations to cause us to stumble.

In fact, we see this principle exemplified in the life of Jesus, the Son of God. Like the first man, Adam, Jesus also faced a test, but with a significant difference. Jesus, the last Adam, was specifically led by the Spirit of God into the wilderness to be tested (Luke 4:1–2). However, it was not God who administered the test but rather the devil himself.

During His time in the wilderness, Jesus encountered various temptations presented by the devil. The devil tried to exploit Jesus' physical hunger, offered Him power and authority over the kingdoms of the world, and even challenged Him to put God's protection to the test. Yet, in each temptation, Jesus responded with the power of God's Word, affirming His unwavering commitment to the Father.

Just as the teacher in our illustration does not manipulate the test results, God did not intervene to prevent Jesus from experiencing temptation. However, Jesus, unlike Adam, triumphed over the test and emerged victorious. He overcame each temptation by relying on the Word of God and His unwavering commitment to the Father's will.

Passing a test or overcoming temptation is a challenging task. Jesus Himself experienced being led by the Holy Spirit to be tempted, and He understood the difficulty involved. When He taught His disciples how to pray, He encouraged them to ask that they would not be led into temptation but delivered from evil (Matthew 6:13). This acknowledgment shows that Jesus was aware of the trials and temptations that could come their way.

However, it is important to note that the absence of tests and temptations in our lives does not imply that we are exempt from them. On the contrary, James exhorts believers to count it all joy when they face various trials, knowing that the testing of their faith produces endurance (James 1:2–3). Trials and temptations serve a purpose in our spiritual growth and development. They challenge us to rely on God, strengthen our faith, and produce endurance within us.

While it is natural to desire deliverance from temptation, Jesus' teaching reveals the significance of asking God to lead us away from situations that may potentially lead us into temptation. It is a plea for divine guidance and protection in our journey of faith. We acknowledge that without God's help, we may be more vulnerable to succumbing to temptation.

After successfully passing the test, Jesus returned from the wilderness in the power of the Holy Spirit (Luke 4:14). His fame spread throughout the region, and His ministry gained even greater impact and authority.

This illustration reminds us that temptations and tests are not sent by God to trip us up or cause us to stumble. Instead, they come from the enemy, who seeks to lure us away from God's path. However, when we face trials and temptations, we can draw strength and guidance from God's Word, just as Jesus did.

Through our reliance on Him, we can overcome and be promoted to new levels of spiritual growth, experiencing the power of the Holy Spirit and making an even greater impact for His kingdom.

Temptation: How it works (Illustrated)

Imagine two hearts, one made of metal and the other made of wood. A heart made of metal is strongly attracted to a powerful magnet. All it takes is to position a metal object near it, and the heart instantly catches onto it. The magnetic force is so strong that the metal heart cannot resist being drawn towards the magnet. On the other hand, the heart made of wood remains unaffected by the magnet, no matter how close it is to the heart.

Now, let's relate this illustration to the concept of a heart subject to lust and temptation. James 1:14–16 (KJV) explains, "But every man is tempted when he is drawn away by his own lust and enticed. Then when lust has conceived, it brings forth sin, and sin, when it is finished, brings forth death. Do not err, my beloved brethren."

In this illustration, the heart made of metal symbolizes a heart that is hardened by sin and subject to lustful desires. Just like the metal heart is easily attracted to the magnet, a heart subject to lust is drawn towards temptations. The magnet represents the enticing allure of worldly desires and sinful pleasures.

However, when the heart is changed from one made of metal to one made of flesh, symbolizing a heart that is transformed and renewed by God's grace, something remarkable happens. As the heart of the flesh begins to love and desire the things of God, it becomes unresponsive to the magnet of temptation.

By setting our affections on things above, as Colossians 3:2 instructs us, the things of the world lose their attractiveness. The magnet of temptation loses its pull, and we are empowered to resist and overcome.

Furthermore, it is important to recognise that the devil is constantly on the lookout for opportunities to devour and tempt believers, just as described in 1 Peter 5:8. He scans our lives, searching for any weaknesses or areas of vulnerability, as represented by the scanning of the hearts. If he finds material within us that resonates with his evil agenda, such as anger, bitterness, or any other sinful inclination, he will exploit it as an entry point for temptation and seek to bring us down.

However, we can learn from Jesus' example. In John 14:30, Jesus confidently declared, "Hereafter I will not talk much with you; for the prince of this world cometh, and hath nothing in me." Jesus understood that the devil could find no foothold in His heart because He was completely surrendered to the will of the Father.

In conclusion, through the transformation of our hearts from a heart of stone to a heart of flesh, by setting our affections on heavenly things, and by allowing the Holy Spirit to renew our minds, we become less susceptible to the allure of temptations. The magnet of temptation loses its grip on our lives, and we can confidently resist the schemes of the devil, remaining steadfast in our faith and walking in victory.

Chapter 14

The Hope of Eternity

Resurrection of the Dead: The Human Body

It is crucial to understand that the human body, also known as the flesh, is what sets man apart. Our physical bodies provide us with a legal basis to exist on Earth. It is through the human body that we have the opportunity for salvation, for once we depart from the body, that opportunity ceases. However, the devil exploited the human body in the Garden of Eden, creating a rival system to that of God. The corruption introduced by the devil resulted in the inability of flesh and blood to inherit the Kingdom of God, as stated in 1 Corinthians 15:50.

Jesus, being God, is known by various names such as the Word, the Son of God, the Prince of Peace, Emmanuel, and more. It is important to recognise that Jesus is a spirit and also a location in the spirit realm. When Jesus rose from the dead, God highly exalted Him and bestowed upon Him a name above all names. Every knee must bow at the name of Jesus, indicating that Jesus is a spiritual location where demonic spirits and devils must submit. The name of the Lord is described as a strong tower, providing safety to the righteous. Therefore, when we come to the Father in prayer, we approach Him through

Jesus. We can "put on" the Lord Jesus as if wearing a garment, and we are seated with Him in heavenly places, as mentioned in Ephesians.

Jesus came to redeem and restore man back to God, and for this purpose, He needed a body. In Hebrews 10:5, it is stated that when Jesus came into the world, He said, "Sacrifice and offering You did not desire, but a body You have prepared for Me." The incarnation of Jesus in human flesh was crucial for Him to legally die for us and take our place. Death, in relation to humans, pertains to the physical body. Spirits cannot die, but when the spirit departs from the body, death occurs. Jesus, being a spirit, needed a body to fulfil the act of dying on our behalf. The body prepared for Christ qualified Him to die for us.

The body of Christ remains a subject of contention, including the concept of the Antichrist. The body of the Lord Jesus Christ, referred to as Christ, represents the anointing or covering of the spirit. Just as anointing involves smearing or covering something with oil, the body of Christ serves as a covering for the spirit of Jesus. This covering grants Him the legal right to die for us. In 1 John 2:22, anyone who denies that Jesus is the Christ, the anointed body, is considered an Antichrist. First John 4:3 and 2 John 1:7 reiterate that anyone who does not confess that Jesus Christ has come in the flesh is a deceiver and an Antichrist. Thus, the body of Jesus plays a significant role in our redemption and resurrection.

In 1 Corinthians 15:3, Paul delivers the message he received, stating that Christ died for our sins according to the Scriptures. It was Christ, not Jesus, who died, emphasising that it was his body that died. The body prepared for Christ qualified him to die for us. As mentioned in verse 4, he was buried and rose again on the third day, according to the Scriptures. It was Christ's body that rose from the dead. The spirit that raised Jesus from the dead can also quicken our mortal bodies, as stated in the same chapter.

Paul continues in 1 Corinthians 15:12, discussing the resurrection from the dead. He questions those who deny the resurrection, stating that if Christ is preached as not rising from the dead, then there is no hope for the resurrection of the dead. In verse 14, he emphasises that if Christ is not raised, then preaching and faith are in vain.

Reiterating his point, Paul asserts in verse 16 that if the dead do not rise, then Christ is not raised. In verse 17, he affirms that if Christ is not raised, faith is futile, and sin remains. However, in verse 20, Paul confidently declares that Christ is risen from the dead and has become the firstfruits of those who have died.

Thus, the message conveyed is that Christ's body, representing the anointing and covering, died and rose again, providing salvation and hope for the resurrection of our mortal bodies.

***

The First Fruits: Every Man in his own Order
When Jesus died and rose from the dead, as mentioned in Matthew 27:51–52, the veil of the temple was torn, the earth quaked, rocks split, and the graves were opened. Many of the bodies of the saints who had fallen asleep were raised and appeared to many in the Holy City after Jesus's resurrection.

In 1 Corinthians 15:35–37, Paul addresses the question of how the dead are raised and with what kind of body they come. He explains that unless a grain of wheat falls to the earth and dies, it remains alone, but when it dies, it produces many fruits. God gives it a body as He pleases, and each seed has its own body.

Paul further explains the nature of the resurrection in verse 42, stating that the dead are raised in incorruption, glory, power, and as a spiritual body. This understanding is evident in the resurrection of those saints who were raised when Jesus died. They died as natural bodies but were raised as spiritual bodies.

Therefore, the message conveyed is that through Jesus's death and resurrection, the saints who were raised experienced a transformation from a natural body to a spiritual body, demonstrating the power and nature of the resurrection.

Before Jesus Christ died, He had physical interactions with people on Earth, such as knocking on doors, eating with Lazarus, and conversing with Zacchaeus. He appeared as a normal human being. However, after Jesus's death, He manifested in a different way. One of His appearances was to Mary Magdalene, as mentioned in Mark 16:9.

The term "appear" is used to describe the manifestation of a dead body or a spiritual being with supernatural abilities. We see this in the case of Elijah and Moses appearing to others, as mentioned in Mark 9:4. Acts 9:17 also speaks of Jesus appearing to Saul (later known as Paul) on his way to Damascus. Similarly, after Jesus's resurrection, people who were raised from the dead appeared to many, as described in Matthew 27:53.

Their appearance indicates a change in their state. Just as Paul states in 1 Corinthians 15:51–52, not all will sleep (die), but all will be changed. They would put on incorruption, transitioning from a corruptible natural body to an incorruptible spiritual body. These resurrected individuals, witnessed by many, were transformed into a new form, different from their previous natural bodies.

However, they did not remain on Earth. As Jesus ascended, the Bible tells us that He ascended on a cloud. These resurrected individuals, I believe, became part of the cloud of witnesses mentioned in Hebrews 12:1. John 3:13 states that no one has ascended to heaven except the Son of Man, who came down from heaven. When Jesus ascended, He took with Him the first fruits—the ones raised from the dead—and they went to heaven.

It is important to note that before Jesus's death, men who died went to a place called the bosom of Abraham. This is different from paradise or heaven. However, after Jesus's death on the cross, salvation took place. As seen in the example of the thief on the cross, who asked Jesus to remember him in His kingdom, Jesus assured him that they would be together in paradise that same day.

Additionally, after Jesus's death, He descended into Hades to preach to the spirits there, as mentioned in 1 Peter 3:18–20. The bosom of Abraham and the place where the rich man was, though referred to as "hell," are actually Hades. The rich man, in his conversation with Abraham, mentions a great chasm separating them, indicating that crossing over was not possible.

These places served as temporary locations for the spirits of the departed. However, I believe that when those who were born again received Jesus's preaching, they left the bosom of Abraham and entered paradise. This is exemplified by the thief on the cross, who was promised paradise by Jesus.

For those who have died in Christ and have been buried, there is a future event awaiting them. As mentioned in 1 Corinthians 15:51-52, there is a mystery revealed: not all will experience physical death, but all will undergo a transformation. In a moment, in the twinkling of an eye, at the last trumpet, the dead will be raised incorruptible. When we speak of the dead in Christ being raised, we refer to their bodies being raised incorruptible, as their spirits already reside in paradise. The body dies, but it will put on a spiritual body. The mortal will be clothed with immortality. This is the promise that the dead in Christ will rise, as the trumpet sounds and they are changed. The corruptible will put on incorruption, and the mortal will put on immortality. Then the saying will come to pass: "Death is swallowed up in victory. O Death, where is your sting? O Grave, where is your victory?" The sting of death is sin, and the power of sin is the law. But thanks be to God, who gives us the victory through our Lord Jesus Christ.

In 1 Thessalonians 4, Paul addresses the believers regarding those who have fallen asleep (died). He urges them not to grieve as those who have no hope. Our hope extends beyond this world. Jesus Christ is the hope of glory. There will be a day when all the bodies that are dead and buried will be changed and raised incorruptible. This is the hope that gives us comfort. Just as we believe that Jesus died and rose again, we also believe that God will bring with Him those who sleep in Jesus. The order of events is revealed: those who are alive will wait for the dead to be changed. The Lord Himself will descend from heaven with a shout, with the voice of an angel, and with the trumpet of God. The dead in Christ will rise first, and then we who are alive and remain will be caught up together with them in the clouds. We will meet the Lord in the air, and we will be with Him forever. Therefore, let us comfort one another with these words.

These words provide assurance and comfort for our loved ones who have died in Christ. Our hope extends beyond this earthly realm, and we will see them again in their glorified bodies. They are part of the first fruits, as Paul mentions in 1 Corinthians 15.

In 1 Corinthians 15:20, it is stated that Christ has risen from the dead and has become the first fruits of those who slept. He became the first fruit of those who died, and those who rose during His resurrection ascended with Him as the first fruits. This was a testament to God, a demonstration of His work in dying for the people. Christ went with the first fruits, those who rose when He died, as evidence of His sacrifice. He became the first fruit of those who slept. Then, in verse 23, it is mentioned that every man will rise in his own order. Christ rose first, followed by the first fruits who were resurrected during His death, burial, and resurrection. Afterward, at Christ's coming, those who belong to Him will also rise. When the trumpet sounds, the dead in Christ, whose spirits currently reside in paradise, will have their bodies transformed into spiritual bodies and be caught up to reunite with their spirits. Then, those of us who are alive will also be changed and caught up to meet them in the clouds, to be with the Lord forever.

This message brings great hope, as it assures us that death is not the end and that we will experience resurrection and glory. We are not destined to remain in the ground and decay forever. The hope of resurrection is something to eagerly anticipate. Paul emphasised this hope in 1 Corinthians 15, urging people to repent and turn to God. He called them to wake up to righteousness and not to continue in sin. For those who lack knowledge of God, it is a matter of shame. Without the righteousness of God and a relationship with Him through Jesus Christ, there is no place in the Kingdom of God. To partake in the resurrection we discussed, one must be born again, receiving the life of Christ and accepting Him as Lord and Saviour. By doing so, one gains the hope of eternal life, the hope of glory, and the assurance of being resurrected and transformed from a corruptible body to an incorruptible body. In this way, we will forever be with the Lord in the air.

***

The Rapture: Our Ark of safety before the impending Judgement

The Rapture is the imminent event where Jesus Christ will come for His church, His bride, to catch them away and meet Him in the air for the marriage supper of the Lamb. Jesus provided two examples from the past to illustrate this event. In Luke 17:26, He compared it to the days of Noah, when people were eating, drinking, marrying, and being given in marriage until the day Noah entered the ark, and the flood came and destroyed them all. Similarly, in verse 28, Jesus mentioned the days of Lot, when people were eating, drinking, buying, selling, planting, and building until the day Lot left Sodom and it rained fire and brimstone, destroying them all. Jesus emphasised that the day of the Son of Man's revelation will be like those days, with a sudden event and judgement.

Why does the church need to be taken out of the way? Second Thessalonians, chapter 2, addresses this question. The passage urges believers not to be deceived or troubled by false reports that the day of Christ is at hand. It clarifies that before that day can come, there must first be a falling away. This refers to a departure from the faith, with many people backsliding and turning away due to the influence of seducing spirits and demonic doctrines. As iniquity abounds and the love of many grows cold, this falling away will occur. The Bible indicates that in the latter times, evil will increase and wicked men will become stronger. Thus, the falling away is a sign that judgement is approaching.

In light of the reference to Noah and Lot, who experienced a great increase in wickedness before judgement came, we can understand the significance of the falling away. Just as people rejected Noah's message and persisted in their evil ways, reaching a point where their hearts were filled with wickedness, judgement befell them. Likewise, the wickedness and backsliding in the days of Lot led to the destruction of Sodom. Thus, the falling away before the day of Christ's revelation is a sign that judgement is imminent.

In the case of Lot, as described in Genesis 18:17–33, we witness a similar pattern. The Bible tells us that God intended to bring judgement upon Sodom and Gomorrah due to their great wickedness and outcry. Abraham, knowing that Lot and his family were in Sodom, approached God and pleaded for the righteous to be spared. He asked if God would destroy the city if fifty righteous people were found, then progressively negotiated the number down to ten.

Abraham recognised that it would be unjust for the righteous to perish with the wicked. God agreed that He would not destroy the city if ten righteous individuals were present. Ultimately, Lot and his family were rescued from the impending judgement, and God rained destruction upon the city.

This account reveals an important principle: God preserves the righteous and provides an escape before unleashing His judgement. If a city or society becomes overwhelmingly corrupt, with only a small remnant of righteous individuals remaining, God will remove the righteous before executing judgement. This was evident in the case of Lot and the cities of Sodom and Gomorrah. When the righteous diminish to a minority and iniquity abounds, God takes action to protect His children and execute judgement upon the wicked.

The same principle applies to the future event of the Rapture. Prior to the Rapture, there will be a significant falling away from the faith, with widespread turning away from God and an increase in evil practices. The world will experience a heightened level of iniquity and a lack of godliness. This decline and moral decay will be disheartening, signifying the approaching judgement. However, before God's judgement is poured out upon the earth, the Rapture will occur as an escape for believers. God will take His children out of the world and bring them to safety in heaven, just as He took Lot and his family out of Sodom before its destruction.

The parallel between the accounts of Noah, Lot, and the future Rapture emphasises God's pattern of rescuing the righteous before executing judgement. In all these instances, God preserved those who remained faithful to Him and provided a way of escape. As believers, we can find hope and reassurance in the knowledge that God will protect and deliver His children before pouring out His judgement upon the world. The Rapture is the ark of safety and deliverance for the righteous, ensuring that they will be spared from the coming judgement.

Second Thessalonians 2:7 reveals the mystery of iniquity, which is already at work. The church, empowered by the Holy Spirit, restrains this iniquity. The church is the one that allows the world to keep operating, keeping destruction at bay. However, when the church is taken out of the way through the Rapture, it will pave the way for God's judgement to be unleashed upon the Earth. The wicked will be revealed, and the Lord will consume them with the spirit of His mouth and destroy them with the brightness of His coming. The coming of the wicked one will be accompanied by the working of Satan, with power, signs, lying wonders, and deceivableness. Those who do not receive the love of the truth and delight in unrighteousness will be deceived and condemned. God will send them strong delusion so that they believe lies and face damnation.

Knowing that Jesus Christ is coming soon, we see the signs around us. This serves as a warning to those who do not yet know Christ. It is essential to accept Him as Lord and Saviour today to avoid being partakers of the impending doom. In 1 Thessalonians 5:1–11, we are reminded that the day of the Lord will come like a thief in the night. However, as children of light, we are not in darkness, and it will not overtake us unexpectedly. Therefore, we must be vigilant, watchful, and sober. We are urged to put on the breastplate of faith and love and the helmet of the hope of salvation. God has not appointed us to wrath but to obtain salvation through our Lord Jesus Christ. We, as children of God, have been given the opportunity to escape the wrath and destruction that await the world. By accepting Jesus Christ as our Lord and personal Saviour, we can find salvation and avoid the appointed judgement.

Study Guides

YOUR STRUCTURED COMPANION IN GAINING A DEEPER UNDERSTANDING OF RESTORED

Study Guide: Chapter 1 – The gap theory and Lucifer's fall and rebellion

Tips for application:

1. Approach the study with an open mind and a desire to understand God's creation and His sovereignty.

2. Remember that the central message of the Bible is about God's creative power, redemption through Jesus Christ, and our response to His grace and love.

3. While the Gap Theory provides an interesting exploration of creation, focus on the foundational teachings and essential truths of Scripture.

Study questions:

1. What does Ecclesiastes 1 verses 9–10 reveal about the timeless nature of the Earth? How does it prompt exploration into the Gap Theory?

2. How does Genesis 1 verses 1 affirm the goodness and perfection of God's creative work? What perplexing description is introduced in Genesis 1 verses 2?

3. What do passages like 1 John 1 verses 5, Isaiah 66 verses 1, and Acts 7 verses 49 reveal about the absence of darkness in God's initial creation?

4. What is the Gap Theory, and how does it propose to explain the transition from a perfect creation to a state of formlessness and void?

5. What are the criticisms of the Gap Theory, and how do some interpret Genesis 1 verses 2 as a state before God's creative actions brought order and beauty to the Earth?

Reflection and application:

1. Reflect on the implications of the Gap Theory and the possible catastrophic event between Genesis 1 verses 1 and 1 verses 2. How does it impact your understanding of creation and God's sovereignty?

2. Consider the importance of maintaining a humble and obedient heart, like that of the angels before Lucifer's fall. How can you apply this principle in your own life?

3. Think about the significance of God's redemptive plan through Jesus Christ. How does this central message of the Bible influence your worldview and interactions with others?

Practical exercise:

1. Read and meditate on the key Scriptures mentioned in the chapter (Ecclesiastes 1 verses 9–10, Genesis 1 verses 1–2, 1 John 1 verses 5, Isaiah 66 verses 1, Acts 7 verses 49, Revelation 21 verses 23, and Revelation 22 verses 5).

2. Engage in a group discussion or study with others to share perspectives on the Gap Theory and its implications. Respectfully consider alternative viewpoints and explore the theological implications together.

Scripture to meditate on:
- Psalm 8 verses 1
- Psalm 50 verses 4
- Psalm 57 verses 5
- Psalm 11
- Ezekiel 28 verses 12–19
- Isaiah 14 verses 12–14

Remember to approach the study with a heart of humility and a desire to grow in your understanding of God's Word. As you delve into these topics, seek to deepen your relationship with God and apply His truths in your life.

Study Guide: Chapter 2 - Restoration of order

Tips for application:

1. Approach the study with a willingness to understand God's restoration of order in the chaotic world.

2. Reflect on the significance of light and darkness, and how they represent spiritual truths in our lives.

3. Consider how God's protection and presence offer comfort and assurance, even in the face of darkness and evil.

Study questions:

1. What caused the earth to become formless, void, and flooded with water in the beginning, and how did God restore order to this chaotic world?

2. How does John 1 verses 3-5 connect Jesus Christ to the light mentioned in Genesis 1 verses 3? What does this light symbolize?

3. What is the significance of God dividing the light from the darkness in Genesis 1 verses 4? How does this relate to the location of Day and Night?

4. How does the concept of light and darkness apply to believers in their daily lives, as mentioned in Ephesians 5 verses 11 and Romans 13 verses 12?

5. What is the importance of recognizing that as children of God, believers are not of darkness, and how does this provide assurance and comfort?

Reflection and application:

1. Reflect on the concept of light as represented by Jesus Christ and its impact on dispelling darkness. How can you actively bring the light of Christ into your life and the lives of others?

2. Consider the activities of devils heightened in the darkness of night. How can you rely on God's protection and trust in His presence during challenging times?

3. Contemplate the idea of God creating man in His own image and likeness. How does this truth shape your understanding of your identity and purpose as a believer?

Practical exercise:

1. Read and meditate on the key Scriptures mentioned in the chapter (Genesis 1 verses 3-4, Matthew 25 verses 41, Ephesians 6 verses 12, Proverbs 18 verses 10, John 16 verses 33, Psalm 23 verses 4, Psalm 127 verses 2, Psalm 91 verses 5, and Genesis 1 verses 26-27).

2. Spend time in prayer, asking God to reveal His light in your life and seeking His protection and presence in times of darkness.

3. Engage in a group discussion or study with others to share insights and reflections on God's restoration of order and His role as the Light in our lives.

Scripture to meditate on:
- John 1 verses 3-5
- Ephesians 5 verses 11
- Romans 13 verses 12
- 1 Thessalonians 5 verses 5
- Psalm 23 verses 4

- Psalm 91 verses 5
- Genesis 1 verses 26-27

Study Guide: Chapter 3 - In the Image of God

Tips for Application:

1. Reflect on the significance of being created in the image of God. Consider how this impacts your identity and purpose as a human being.

2. Meditate on the triune nature of man - spirit, soul, and body. Understand how they work together and how the soul serves as a mediator between the spirit and the body.

3. Embrace the privilege of having a physical body (flesh) as a qualification to receive the outpouring of God's Spirit. Utilize your physical body to glorify God and fulfill His purposes on earth.

Study Questions:

1. What does it mean to be created in the image of God? How does this concept influence your understanding of your identity and purpose?

2. Explain the two distinct parts of man's creation as described in Genesis 1:26 and 1:27. How does this reflect the triune nature of man?

3. What evidence from Scripture supports the belief that man's spirit existed before physical formation? How does this highlight the eternal nature of human beings?

4. Describe the role of the soul in the triune composition of man. How does the soul serve as a mediator between the spirit and the body?

5. How does David's example in the Psalms illustrate the relationship between the spirit, soul, and body? How did he find strength in the Lord during times of distress?

Reflection and Application:

1. Reflect on the role of the Holy Spirit in enlivening the soul and imparting spiritual life. How can you actively yield to the Holy Spirit to lead and guide your life?

2. Consider the value of your physical body as a qualification to receive God's Spirit and experience salvation. How does this perspective change your view of your flesh?

3. Evaluate your understanding of the flesh and its influence on your spiritual journey. How can you avoid the negative aspects of the flesh while utilizing it for God's purposes?

Practical Exercise:

1. Spend time in prayer and meditation, seeking the guidance of the Holy Spirit in your life. Ask Him to enliven your soul and empower you to live in righteousness.

2. Reflect on specific areas of your life where you can use your physical body (flesh) as a tool for advancing your spiritual journey and glorifying God. Set goals to implement these changes.

Scripture to Meditate on:

1. Genesis 1:26-27 - Then God said, "Let us make mankind in our image, in our likeness..." So God created mankind in his own image, in the image of God he created them; male and female he created them.

2. John 4:24 - God is spirit, and his worshipers must worship in the Spirit and in truth.

3. Acts 17:28 - For in him we live and move and have our being. As some of your own poets have said, 'We are his offspring.'

4. Romans 12:2 - Do not conform to the pattern of this world, but be transformed by the renewing of your mind. Then you will be able to test and approve what God's will is—his good, pleasing, and perfect will.

5. 1 Corinthians 6:19 - Do you not know that your bodies are temples of the Holy Spirit, who is in you, whom you have received from God? You are not your own.

Study Guide: Chapter 4 - The Flesh, The World, and The Devil

Tips for Application:

1. Recognize the tactics of the devil: Understand the devil's schemes to deceive and tempt you away from God's purpose for your life.

2. Shift your focus from the flesh: Learn from Jesus' example in overcoming temptation by focusing on the Spirit and God's Word rather than on immediate physical desires.

3. Reject the world's allure: Be cautious of the world's systems and temptations that lead you away from God's will and righteousness.

4. Worship God alone: Resist the devil's desire for worship and instead, worship the one true God by obeying His commands.

Study Questions:

1. What was the devil's plan after his unsuccessful attempt to exalt himself above God?

2. How did the devil deceive humanity into embracing the realm of the Flesh?

3. What are the three benefits the devil obtained through the fall of humanity?

4. How did Jesus respond to the devil's temptations in the wilderness?

5. What is the distinction between the world and the earth?

6. How did the devil gain authority over the kingdoms of the world?

7. What is the devil's ultimate agenda, and how does he seek worship?

Reflection and Application:

1. Reflect on how the concept of the Flesh affects your daily life and decisions. Identify areas where you need to shift your focus from the flesh to the Spirit.

2. Consider the allure of the world's systems and its potential impact on your relationship with God. Evaluate your priorities and make necessary adjustments to put God first.

3. Examine areas of your life where the devil may be attempting to deceive you. Develop strategies to resist his lies and stay aligned with God's truth.

4. Meditate on the consequences of worshipping anything or anyone other than God. Renew your commitment to worshipping God alone in spirit and truth.

Practical Exercise:

1. Take time for personal prayer and reflection. Ask God to reveal any areas of your life where you may be falling into the trap of the Flesh, the World, or the Devil.

2. Choose a passage from the Scripture provided in the chapter (e.g., Luke 4:3-4, 1 John 2:15-16, Revelation 13:4) and memorize it. Use it as a reminder to resist temptation and focus on God.

3. Identify a specific area of your life where the world's systems are influencing your decisions. Seek wise counsel and develop a plan to realign your priorities with God's will.

Scripture to Meditate on:

Galatians 5:17 - "For the flesh lusteth against the Spirit, and the Spirit against the flesh: and these are contrary the one to the other: so that ye cannot do the things that ye would."

1 Timothy 6:10 - "For the love of money is the root of all evil: which while some coveted after, they have erred from the faith, and pierced themselves through with many sorrows."

1 John 2:15 - "Love not the world, neither the things that are in the world. If any man love the world, the love of the Father is not in him."

Luke 4:8 - "And Jesus answered and said unto him, Get thee behind me, Satan: for it is written, Thou shalt worship the Lord thy God, and him only shalt thou serve."

Revelation 13:4 - "And they worshipped the dragon which gave power unto the beast: and they worshipped the beast, saying, Who is like unto the beast? who is able to make war with him?"

Study Guide: Chapter 5 – The Fall and Death of the Living Soul

Tips for Application:

1. Understand the consequences of sin: Recognise that sin leads to death and separation from God's intended plan for our lives.

2. Seek spiritual connection: Strive to reconnect with God's Spirit and align yourself with His will to experience an abundant life.

3. Guard against temptation: Be vigilant against the devil's deceitful tactics and focus on God's truth to resist temptation.

4. Embrace God's redemption plan: Trust in God's plan of redemption through Jesus Christ and seek forgiveness for sin.

Study Questions:

1. What was God's intention in giving Adam a clear command with consequences?

2. How did the devil tempt Eve to sin against God?

3. What are the stages of death experienced by man as a triune being?

4. How does the devil manipulate the soul to gain control over man?

5. How did God's Spirit sustain man's soul before the fall?

6. Why did God establish a redemption plan even before man's fall?

7. How does physical death result from the fall of man?

Reflection and Application:

1. Reflect on the consequences of the fall of man and how it affects your own life. Acknowledge areas where sin has caused separation from God.

2. Examine the workings of temptation in your life and identify strategies to resist the devil's deceitful tactics.

3. Consider the significance of seeking spiritual connection with God's Spirit to experience an abundant life. How can you deepen your relationship with God?

4. Meditate on God's redemption plan through Jesus Christ. Embrace the forgiveness and restoration offered through Him.

Practical Exercise:

1. Engage in personal prayer and seek forgiveness for areas of sin in your life. Ask for guidance in reconnecting with God's Spirit.

2. Journal your reflections on the stages of death experienced by man as a triune being. Identify areas in your life where you may be experiencing death and separation from God.

3. Memorise Scriptures that emphasise the consequences of sin and the hope of redemption through Jesus Christ.

Scripture to Meditate on:

Genesis 2:17 - "But of the tree of the knowledge of good and evil, thou shalt not eat of it: for in the day that thou eatest thereof thou shalt surely die."

James 1:15 - "Then when lust hath conceived, it bringeth forth sin: and sin, when it is finished, bringeth forth death."

John 15:6 - "If a man abide not in me, he is cast forth as a branch, and is withered; and men gather them, and cast them into the fire, and they are burned."

2 Peter 3:8 - "But, beloved, be not ignorant of this one thing, that one day is with the Lord as a thousand years, and a thousand years as one day."

Study Guide: Chapter 6 - The Corrupted Soul and God's Displeasure

Tips for Application:

1. Recognise the importance of prayer as a means of communication with God and invite Him into your daily affairs.

2. Understand the impact of corruption and the alternate system on humanity's ability to seek God and commune with Him.

3. Embrace the message of repentance and God's mercy, accepting Jesus Christ as your Lord and Saviour to secure your eternal well-being.

4. Be vigilant in prayer, relying on the Holy Spirit's guidance to overcome the weaknesses of the flesh and resist temptation.

5. Seek alignment with God's original design and purposes, realising the limitations of the flesh without a connection to the Spirit.

Study Questions:

1. How did the fall of man lead to the emergence of the flesh as an alternate system, and what impact did this have on humanity's communication with God?

2. How did Satan's corrupting influence affect the thoughts and intentions of man's heart, leading to a state of continuous evil?

3. What role does prayer play in inviting God into our lives, and how does the Holy Spirit assist us in this spiritual discipline?

4. Explain God's repentance and mercy as demonstrated in His covenant after the flood and the symbolism of the rainbow.

5. What are the consequences of corruption on the human lifespan, and how did this misalignment separate man from God's original design?

Reflection and Application:

1. Reflect on your prayer life and identify areas where you can be more watchful and persistent in seeking God's guidance through the Holy Spirit.

2. Consider the impact of corruption on humanity and recognise the need for repentance and acceptance of Jesus Christ as your Saviour.

3. Meditate on God's mercy and grace as demonstrated in His covenant after the flood, and embrace the promise of His enduring love for all living creatures.

4. Take time to contemplate the symbolism of the rainbow and its reminder of God's faithfulness and commitment to His promises.

5. Assess your alignment with God's purposes and seek to deepen your connection with Him through the indwelling of the Holy Spirit.

Practical Exercise:

1. Set aside dedicated time for prayer each day, seeking the guidance of the Holy Spirit in your communication with God.

2. Study passages that highlight God's mercy and repentance, and create a personal prayer of thanksgiving for His love and grace.

3. Spend time in nature, observing rainbows or other signs of God's covenant, and use these moments to meditate on His faithfulness.

4. Engage in self-examination, identifying areas of your life where corruption and misalignment may have hindered your relationship with God, and commit to repentance and realignment.

5. Share your reflections and experiences with a trusted friend or mentor, encouraging each other in your journey of seeking God and living in alignment with His purposes.

Scripture to Meditate on: Genesis 9:13-16 - "I do set my bow in the cloud, and it shall be for a token of a covenant between me and the earth. And it shall come to pass, when I bring a cloud over the earth, that the bow shall be seen in the cloud. And I will remember my covenant, which is between me and you and every living creature of all flesh; and the waters shall no more become a flood to destroy all flesh. And the bow shall be in the cloud, and I will look upon it, that I may remember the everlasting covenant between God and every living creature of all flesh that is upon the earth."

Study Guide: Chapter 7 – The Law as a Schoolmaster

Tips for Application:

1. Recognise your sinful nature: Understand that we are all born with a sinful nature inherited from Adam, making it impossible for us to please God in our own strength.

2. Embrace the purpose of the law: See the law as a schoolmaster that reveals our need for salvation through faith in Christ, not as a means of achieving righteousness on our own.

3. Rely on Christ's righteousness: Trust in Jesus as the only source of true righteousness and salvation. Our works and efforts cannot justify us before God.

4. Cultivate humility: Acknowledge the inadequacy of human efforts and self-righteousness. Humbly submit to God's righteousness and grace.

5. Embrace the ministry of the Holy Spirit: Allow the Spirit to guide and transform your life, enabling you to walk in righteousness and live according to God's will.

Study Questions:

1. How did the fall of man affect humanity's ability to please God?
2. Why did God give the law, and what was its purpose?

3. What role does the law play in revealing our need for salvation through Christ?

4. How does the law point us towards Christ as the ultimate solution to our spiritual predicament?

5. What are the dangers of self-righteousness and relying solely on human efforts for salvation?

6. In what ways can we apply the concept of the law as a schoolmaster in our daily lives?

Reflection and Application: Reflect on your own journey of faith and how you once viewed the law and righteousness. Consider how your understanding has changed after learning about the law's purpose and its role in pointing us to Christ. Think about areas in your life where you may have relied on self-righteousness or human efforts rather than trusting in Christ's righteousness. How can you shift your focus to fully rely on Him for justification and salvation?

Practical Exercise: Take time to meditate on the passages mentioned in the chapter, such as Romans 3:23, Galatians 2:16, and Romans 10:4. Reflect on how these verses emphasise the inadequacy of human efforts for righteousness and the necessity of faith in Christ. Consider memorising one or more of these verses to keep them close to your heart and mind.

Scripture to Meditate on: Galatians 3:24-25 - "So then, the law was our guardian until Christ came, in order that we might be justified by faith. But now that faith has come, we are no longer under a guardian."

Romans 3:20 - "For by works of the law no human being will be justified in his sight, since through the law comes knowledge of sin."

Romans 7:6 - "But now we are released from the law, having died to that which held us captive, so that we serve in the new way of the Spirit and not in the old way of the written code."

Galatians 3:11 - "Now it is evident that no one is justified before God by the law, for 'The righteous shall live by faith.'"

Closing Prayer: Heavenly Father, thank you for revealing to me the purpose of the law and its role in pointing me towards Christ. Help me to recognise my sinful nature and to humbly rely on Jesus for righteousness and salvation. I surrender my self-righteousness and human efforts, trusting in the ministry of the Holy Spirit to guide and transform my life. In Jesus' name, amen.

Study Guide: Chapter 8 - Jesus Christ: The Restorer of the Living Soul

Tips for Application:

1. Understand the significance of Jesus' sacrifice: Jesus' death on the cross is the ultimate sacrifice that cleanses us from sin and reconciles us with God. Reflect on the power of His blood to bring salvation and forgiveness to those who believe in Him.

2. Embrace God's call to repentance: God's forbearance in the past allowed room for ignorance, but now He calls everyone to repent and turn away from sin. Acknowledge your past shortcomings and seek God's purpose for your life.

3. Strive for perfection through faith: Jesus fulfilled the law on our behalf, and now we are called to live a life that surpasses mere religious observance. Rely on the finished work of Jesus and strive for perfection through a personal relationship with Him.

Study Questions:

1. What were the symbolic provisions for forgiveness of sins in the Old Testament, and why were they insufficient to permanently cleanse sins?

2. Why did God make temporary concessions and allowances under the law, and how were these concessions meant to guide and teach humanity?

3. Give examples of some concessions made under the law, and explain why they were limited to the period of learning.

4. How did Jesus fulfil the law and what higher expectations did He set for believers in the New Testament?

5. How did Jesus address issues like anger, adultery, and divorce in the New Testament, and what does this reveal about the call for perfection?

Reflection and Application:

1. Reflect on the depth of God's goodness, forbearance, and long-suffering towards humanity. How does understanding His forbearance in the past influence your attitude towards repentance and striving for perfection?

2. Examine areas of your life where you may have relied on past concessions or excuses. How can you align yourself with the price Jesus paid for you and seek perfection through faith in Him?

3. Meditate on the concept of Jesus as the ultimate Restorer of the Living Soul. How does His sacrificial death impact your understanding of salvation and reconciliation with God?

Practical Exercise:

1. Read and study the passages from Matthew 5 (verses 17-48) that outline Jesus' expectations for believers in the New Testament. Reflect on how these teachings challenge you to live a life that exceeds religious observance.

2. Engage in prayer and self-examination to identify areas of your life that require repentance and transformation. Ask for the guidance and strength of the Holy Spirit to help you align with God's expectations.

Scripture to Meditate on: Romans 5:8 - "But God demonstrates his own love for us in this: While we were still sinners, Christ died for us."

1 Peter 2:21 - "To this you were called, because Christ suffered for you, leaving you an example, that you should follow in his steps."

Hebrews 10:14 - "For by one sacrifice he has made perfect forever those who are being made holy."

Study Guide: Chapter 9 – The Rebirth of the Living Soul

Tips for Application:

1. Embrace the work of the Holy Spirit in your life and seek to have a deeper fellowship with Him.

2. Recognise the interdependence of your spirit, soul, and body, and strive to align them with God's Word.

3. Engage in regular Bible study and prayer to transform your soul and grow in spiritual maturity.

4. Crucify the flesh daily and manage your body to live a life of victory over sin and temptation.

5. Reflect on the three stages of salvation and assess where you are in your spiritual journey.

Study Questions:

1. What role did the Holy Spirit play in Jesus' life and ministry?

2. Explain the distribution of the life of Christ from the Spirit to the body using the triune structure of man.

3. What are the three stages of salvation, and how do they relate to the stages of death?

4. How does the Holy Spirit work in our souls to bring about transformation and alignment with God's Word?

5. What is the significance of managing and crucifying the body in the process of salvation?

Reflection and Application:

1. Reflect on your understanding of the Holy Spirit's role in your life. Are you actively seeking His fellowship and guidance?

2. Consider how your thoughts, emotions, and actions align with God's Word. Are there areas where you need to surrender to the Holy Spirit's influence?

3. In what ways can you use the spiritual gifts the Holy Spirit has given you to edify the body of Christ?

4. Think about the challenges you face in managing and subduing the desires of the flesh. How can you partner with the Holy Spirit to overcome them?

5. Meditate on the truth of the three stages of salvation and the ultimate transformation of your body. How does this encourage you in your faith journey?

Practical Exercise:

1. Spend time in prayer, asking the Holy Spirit to reveal areas of your life that need transformation and alignment with God's Word.

2. Create a daily routine that includes Bible study and prayer to nurture your spirit and soul.

3. Identify specific areas of your body's corrupt nature that need to be managed and submit them to the Holy Spirit's control.

4. Engage in a local church or small group to exercise your spiritual gifts and contribute to the body of Christ.

5. Journal your reflections and experiences throughout this study and take note of how the Holy Spirit is working in your life.

Study guide: Chapter 10 – Bearing the image of Adam

Section 1: Tips for Application

1. Set aside regular time for personal study and reflection on the concept of bearing the image of the last Adam.

2. Approach this study with a willingness to be transformed and renewed in your mind by the Spirit of God.

3. Keep a journal to record your insights, questions, and personal reflections as you delve into the topic.

4. Engage in prayer, seeking the Holy Spirit's guidance and revelation as you study God's Word.

5. Share your learnings and experiences with fellow believers to encourage and learn from one another in the process.

Section 2: Study Questions

1. What does it mean to "bear the image of the last Adam," and why is this identity essential for believers?

2. How does the process of beholding Jesus in our lives lead to transformation and Christlikeness?

3. Compare and contrast the first Adam's creation and fall with the last Adam's role in restoring humanity to God.

4. Explain the significance of the spiritual birth and being "born again" in the process of reconciliation and transformation.

5. How does the ongoing process of transformation differ from the automatic likeness of the first Adam before the fall?

Section 3: Reflection and Application Take time to meditate on the following questions and apply the insights to your personal journey of bearing the image of the last Adam:

1. Reflect on how your identity as a believer is now rooted in Christ, the last Adam. How does this identity shape your understanding of yourself and your purpose?

2. Consider areas in your life where you need to focus on beholding Jesus more consistently. How can you intentionally seek His presence and character in those areas?

3. Think about the significance of your spiritual birth and being born again. How has this transformation impacted your life, thoughts, and actions?

4. In what ways can you actively cooperate with the Holy Spirit to allow the process of transformation to continue in your life?

5. Share your journey of transformation with a close friend or small group, seeking encouragement and accountability in becoming more Christlike.

Section 4: Practical Exercise

1. Create a daily habit of setting aside time for prayer and meditation on God's Word, focusing on passages that reveal Christ's character and teachings.

2. Choose a specific attribute of Jesus (e.g., love, humility, compassion) to intentionally practice in your interactions with others.

3. Engage in worship and praise, directing your focus on the glory and beauty of the last Adam, Jesus Christ.

4. Memorise and meditate on 2 Corinthians 3:18 to internalise the transformative power of beholding the glory of the Lord.

5. Seek out opportunities to share your testimony of transformation with others, testifying to the work of the last Adam in your life.

Section 5: Scripture to Meditate on

· 1 Corinthians 15:49 (NLT) - "Just as we are now like the earthly man, we will someday be like the heavenly man."

· 2 Corinthians 3:18 - "As we are beholding the glory of the Lord, we are being transformed into the same image from glory to glory, just as by the Spirit of the Lord."

· John 3:3 - "Unless one is born again, he cannot see the kingdom of God."

· John 3:6 - "That which is born of the flesh is flesh, and that which is born of the Spirit is spirit."

Remember that bearing the image of the last Adam is a continual process that requires intentional effort and surrender to the work of the Holy Spirit. May you grow in Christlikeness and reflect His glory in your life.

The Process of Spiritual Growth and Transformation

Section 1: Tips for Application

1. Embrace the journey of spiritual growth with patience and commitment, understanding that it is a gradual process.

2. Develop a habit of regularly meditating on God's Word and seeking the nourishment it provides for your spiritual growth.

3. Be open to embracing the life of the spirit, even when it may not offer instant gratification or visible changes.

4. Cultivate spiritual resilience by trusting in God's power and staying steadfast in times of challenges and setbacks.

5. Seek the guidance of the Holy Spirit in your growth process, allowing Him to transform you into the image of Christ.

Section 2: Study Questions

1. Why is spiritual growth essential for believers, and how does it differ from the instant gratification offered by worldly pursuits?

2. How can the analogy of healthy eating versus junk food help us understand the significance of embracing the life of the spirit?

3. What are some common challenges and temptations that spiritual infants may face in their growth process, and how can they be overcome?

4. How does spiritual resilience develop as we grow in Christ, and why is it crucial for our journey of transformation?

5. Reflect on the concept of becoming children of God and being fully conformed to the image of God. How does this transformation occur in the growth process?

Section 3: Reflection and Application

1. Consider your own spiritual journey and growth. What are some areas where you have experienced growth, and what challenges have you faced along the way?

2. Reflect on times when you may have been tempted by the allure of instant gratification or worldly pursuits. How can you refocus your priorities on spiritual growth?

3. Think about instances in your life when you needed spiritual resilience to overcome challenges. How did your faith in God's power sustain you?

4. Meditate on the concept of being children of God and growing into the image of God. How can this understanding shape your identity and purpose in Christ?

5. Take time to pray and seek the Holy Spirit's guidance in areas where you desire further growth and transformation.

Section 4: Practical Exercise

1. Set aside dedicated time each day for prayer, meditation, and reading God's Word to nourish your spiritual growth.

2. Keep a journal to track your reflections, insights, and progress in your journey of transformation.

3. Practise resilience by facing challenges with faith and trust in God's power to help you overcome them.

4. Engage in worship and praise to focus on God's greatness and cultivate a deeper connection with Him.

5. Find a mentor or spiritual accountability partner to support and encourage you in your growth process.

Section 5: Scripture to Meditate on

· 1 Peter 2:2 - "As newborn babes, desire the pure milk of the word, that you may grow thereby."

· John 1:12 - "But as many as received Him, to them He gave the right to become children of God, to those who believe in His name."

· 2 Corinthians 3:18 - "But we all, with unveiled face, beholding as in a mirror the glory of the Lord, are being transformed into the same image from glory to glory, just as by the Spirit of the Lord."

· Luke 5:39 - "No man also, having drunk old wine straightway, desireth new; for he saith, The old is better."

Remember that spiritual growth is a lifelong process that requires perseverance and dependence on the Holy Spirit. Embrace the transformative journey, knowing that as you grow in Christlikeness, you will experience a deeper connection with God and a more abundant life in Him.

Active Participation in the Process of Restoration

Section 1: Tips for Application

1. Understand that the process of restoration and transformation takes time and active participation.

2. Seek God's presence and guidance through prayer and meditation on His Word to align your thoughts, attitudes, and actions with His truth.

3. Embrace the journey of sanctification and be patient with yourself as you grow in Christlikeness.

4. Be resilient in your faith, trusting in God's power and grace to overcome challenges and temptations.

5. Continuously learn from Jesus and follow His example of meekness and humility in your Christian walk.

Section 2: Study Questions

1. What can we learn from the incident involving Moses and the tablets of the Ten Commandments about our participation in the process of restoration?

2. How does the story of Takwana and the kind counsellor illustrate the positional and progressive aspects of salvation and sanctification?

3. Why is active participation necessary for believers to grow and become the Image of God (Christlikeness)?

4. What role does God play in the process of restoration, and how can we cooperate with Him in this journey?

5. Reflect on the significance of resilience and the willingness to walk in the Spirit in your pursuit of spiritual maturity.

Section 3: Reflection and Application

1. Take time to reflect on your own spiritual journey and growth. What areas have you seen progress in, and where do you feel you still need to actively participate in the restoration process?

2. Consider times when you have experienced the positional aspect of salvation (forgiveness and justification) and the progressive aspect (ongoing growth and sanctification). How can you apply the lessons from these experiences to your current walk with God?

3. Reflect on the role of resilience in your faith. How can you strengthen your trust in God's power and grace to overcome challenges and temptations?

4. Meditate on Jesus' example of meekness and humility. How can you incorporate these traits into your daily life to align with Christ's character?

5. Take a moment to evaluate how much you actively participate in seeking God's presence and guidance in your life. What steps can you take to deepen your relationship with Him?

Section 4: Practical Exercise

1. Develop a daily habit of prayer and meditation on God's Word to seek His presence and guidance in your life.

2. Keep a journal to track your progress in the process of restoration and transformation. Write down your reflections, challenges, and moments of spiritual growth.

3. Practice resilience by turning to God and relying on His strength when facing difficulties or temptations.

4. Seek out opportunities to learn from Jesus and study His teachings to align your life with His truth.

5. Engage in acts of meekness and humility, such as serving others and putting their needs before your own.

Section 5: Scripture to Meditate on

· Exodus 34:1 (ESV) - "The Lord said to Moses, 'Cut for yourself two tablets of stone like the first, and I will write on the tablets the words that were on the first tablets, which you broke.'"

· Matthew 11:28-29 - "Come to me, all who labour and are heavy laden, and I will give you rest. Take my yoke upon you, and learn from me, for I am gentle and lowly in heart, and you will find rest for your souls."

· Galatians 5:16 - "I say then: Walk in the Spirit, and you shall not fulfil the lust of the flesh."

· Philippians 2:13 - "For it is God who works in you, both to will and to work for his good pleasure."

• Romans 8:14 - "For as many as are led by the Spirit of God, these are sons of God."

Remember that active participation in the process of restoration and transformation is essential for your growth as a believer. Embrace the journey with patience, resilience, and a desire to align your life with Christ's character. As you cooperate with God and seek His guidance, you will experience a deeper relationship with Him and a greater likeness to the Image of God.

The Journey of Sanctification: Complementing Salvation for Spiritual Maturity and Victory Over Sin

Section 1: Tips for Application

1. Understand the distinction between salvation and sanctification. Salvation covers the legal penalty of sin, while sanctification is the ongoing process of growing in holiness and victory over sin.

2. Prioritise engaging with the Word of God to nourish your soul and quench your hunger for sin.

3. Embrace sanctification as a transformative journey that requires your active participation and cooperation with the Holy Spirit.

4. Meditate on Scriptures that emphasise the power and importance of God's Word in the process of sanctification.

5. Cultivate a hunger for holiness and purity, seeking to reflect the character of Christ in your daily life.

Section 2: Study Questions

1. How does the analogy of a hungry person receiving payment for a meal relate to the concept of salvation?

2. What is sanctification, and why is it necessary for spiritual maturity and victory over sin?

3. How does Jesus play a role in our sanctification, and what resources has He provided to facilitate this process?

4. What are the benefits of actively engaging with the Word of God in the journey of sanctification?

5. Reflect on the idea of transformation through sanctification. How does this process lead to a life of holiness and purity?

Section 3: Reflection and Application

1. Take time to reflect on your understanding of salvation and sanctification. Do you fully grasp the significance of both aspects in your spiritual walk?

2. Consider your appetite for God's Word. How can you cultivate a deeper hunger for the Scriptures and actively engage with them to experience sanctification?

3. Reflect on the power of God's Word to transform your life. Are there specific areas where you need to allow the Word to penetrate and shape your thoughts and actions?

4. Meditate on the outcome of sanctification described in Ephesians 5:27. How does this inspire you to pursue holiness and purity in your life?

5. Ask the Holy Spirit to guide you in the journey of sanctification. Surrender any areas of resistance and be open to His work in renewing your mind and conforming you to the image of Christ.

Section 4: Practical Exercise

1. Develop a daily habit of reading and meditating on Scripture. Use a Bible reading plan or devotional guide to immerse yourself in God's Word regularly.

2. Keep a journal to record insights and revelations you receive from the Scriptures. Write down areas where you sense the need for sanctification and ask for God's guidance in those areas.

3. Practice memorising key verses that address specific struggles or areas of temptation in your life. Use these verses as weapons against the enemy's attacks.

4. Seek accountability and support from fellow believers in your journey of sanctification. Share your struggles and victories, and pray for one another's growth in holiness.

5. Engage in worship and prayer as a means to draw near to God and invite His presence to transform your heart and mind.

Section 5: Scripture to Meditate on

· Ephesians 5:25-26 (ESV) - "Husbands, love your wives, as Christ loved the church and gave himself up for her, that he might sanctify her, having cleansed her by the washing of water with the word."

· Hebrews 4:12 (ESV) - "For the word of God is living and active, sharper than any two-edged sword, piercing to the division of soul and of spirit, of joints and of marrow, and discerning the thoughts and intentions of the heart."

· Ephesians 5:27 (ESV) - "so that he might present the church to himself in splendour, without spot or wrinkle or any such thing, that she might be holy and without blemish."

Embrace the transformative journey of sanctification and allow God's Word to nourish your soul, leading you to spiritual maturity and victory over sin. Engage actively with the Scriptures and rely on the power of the Holy Spirit to shape you into the likeness of Christ. As you participate in this process, you will experience the fullness of God's sanctifying work in your life.

The Journey of Transformation: Becoming Like Christ

Section 1: Tips for Application

1. Set aside dedicated time for personal study and reflection on the topic of transformation and Christlikeness.

2. Approach this study with an open heart and a willingness to surrender to God's transforming work in your life.

3. Keep a journal to record your thoughts, insights, and personal reflections as you progress through the study.

4. Engage in regular prayer, seeking the Holy Spirit's guidance and empowerment in your journey of transformation.

5. Share your learnings and experiences with fellow believers to encourage one another in the process.

Section 2: Study Questions

1. What is the purpose of Jesus' coming to earth, and how does it relate to our transformation into His likeness?

2. How does actively engaging our minds and hearts play a crucial role in the process of becoming like Christ?

3. In what ways can we cultivate a hunger and thirst for righteousness, leading us to a deeper relationship with Christ?

4. What does it mean to "sow to the Spirit" in the process of transformation, and how can we practically apply this concept in our lives?

5. How can we avoid complacency and actively participate in the transformative journey, understanding the grace and empowerment God provides?

6. What qualities of Christ's mind, as mentioned in Philippians 2:5-10, should we embrace and adopt in our own lives?

Section 3: Reflection and Application Take time to meditate on the following questions and apply the insights to your personal journey of transformation:

1. Reflect on specific areas in your life where you need to actively engage your mind and heart in the process of becoming like Christ.

2. Consider instances where you have experienced God's transforming work, and how it has shaped your character and actions.

3. Think about times when you faced challenges or complacency in your spiritual growth. How can you overcome these obstacles?

4. In what ways can you demonstrate humility, submission, and sacrifice in your daily life, following Christ's example?

5. How can you develop a consistent focus on Christ and His ultimate goal for your life, amidst the distractions of the world?

Section 4: Practical Exercise

1. Memorise and meditate on Philippians 2:5-8 to internalise Christ's mindset of humility and sacrifice.

2. Identify areas in your life where you struggle to yield your mind and heart to God's transformative work. Develop specific prayers to surrender those areas to Him.

3. Engage in regular reading and study of God's Word, focusing on passages that reveal Christ's character and nature.

4. Commit to acts of service and selflessness, reflecting Christ's sacrificial love towards others.

5. Share your journey of transformation with a close friend or accountability partner, encouraging one another in your pursuit of Christlikeness.

Section 5: Scripture to Meditate on

- Philippians 2:5-8 (The mindset of Christ's humility and sacrifice)
- Romans 12:2 (Renewing of the mind)
- Matthew 5:6 (Blessed are those who hunger and thirst for righteousness)
- Galatians 6:8 (Sowing to the Spirit)
- 2 Thessalonians 3:10 (He who does not work should not eat)

Remember, the journey of becoming like Christ is a lifelong process. Embrace it with humility, dedication, and a desire to draw closer to Him. May the Holy Spirit guide and empower you as you seek to reflect the image of the Last Adam in your life.

Study Guide: Chapter 11 - Identifying with Christ's Sufferings

Section 1: Tips for Application

1. Understand the significance of Jesus as our model and example in the journey of sanctification.

2. Embrace the transformative power of Christ's sacrifice on the cross and its impact on your salvation and sanctification.

3. Meditate on the examples Jesus left through His humility, sacrifice, and obedience to God's will.

4. Cultivate a mindset of humility and willingness to suffer for the sake of Christ, knowing that there is a reward in glorification.

5. Commit to daily following Jesus, denying yourself, taking up your cross, and walking in His footsteps.

Section 2: Study Questions

1. What is the distinction between Jesus and us concerning sin, and how does His sacrifice on the cross bring us onto a level playing field with Him?

2. Why did Jesus go to the cross, and how does His death demonstrate the possibilities of transformation and sanctification in our lives?

3. What are some examples of Jesus's humility and obedience to God's will that we are called to imitate in our lives?

4. How does having the same mindset as Christ regarding suffering enable us to experience exaltation and glorification?

5. Reflect on Luke 9:23, "If anyone desires to come after Me, let him deny himself, and take up his cross daily, and follow Me." How can you practically apply this instruction in your daily walk with Christ?

Section 3: Reflection and Application

1. Reflect on the transformative power of Christ's sacrifice on the cross and how it has impacted your life.

2. Consider areas in your life where you can demonstrate greater humility and obedience to God's will, following Jesus's example.

3. Meditate on the rewards and exaltation that come through sacrifice and suffering for the sake of Christ.

4. Reflect on the daily commitment to deny yourself, take up your cross, and follow Jesus. How can you live this out practically in your daily decisions and actions?

5. Ask the Holy Spirit to strengthen and empower you to identify with Christ's sufferings and imitate His character and actions in your life.

Section 4: Practical Exercise

1. Create a daily habit of studying the life and teachings of Jesus in the Gospels. Note specific examples of His humility, sacrifice, and obedience to apply in your life.

2. Keep a journal to record instances where you have experienced transformation and sanctification through identifying with Christ's sufferings.

3. Seek opportunities to serve others with selfless love and compassion, imitating Jesus's example of sacrificial service.

4. Practise daily surrendering your will to God and seeking to align your actions with His Word and teachings.

5. Share your experiences and insights with fellow believers, encouraging one another in the journey of identifying with Christ's sufferings.

Section 5: Scripture to Meditate on

· Romans 8:29 - "For whom He foreknew, He also predestined to be conformed to the image of His Son, that He might be the firstborn among many brethren."

· Philippians 2:5-7 - "Let this mind be in you, which was also in Christ Jesus, who, being in the form of God, did not consider it robbery to be equal with God, but made Himself of no reputation, taking the form of a bondservant and coming in the likeness of men."

· Philippians 2:9 - "Therefore God also has highly exalted Him and given Him the name which is above every name."

Identify with Christ's sufferings and follow His example of humility, sacrifice, and obedience. Embrace the transformative power of Christ's sacrifice on the cross, and allow it to bring about sanctification and glorification in your life. Commit to daily following Jesus and imitating His character and actions as you walk the path of spiritual growth and maturity.

Study Guide: Chapter 12 - Our Spirituality

The relationship between the spirit and the flesh

Tips for Application:

1. Embrace the New Birth: Before focusing on spiritual growth, be certain of your spiritual rebirth and the presence of the Holy Spirit within you.

2. Allow the Spirit to Lead: Instead of adapting the Spirit to the flaws of the flesh, surrender to the leading of the Holy Spirit for transformation and renewal.

3. Seek Identity in Christ: Understand that your true identity is found in Christ, and your physical body does not define your spiritual self.

Study Questions:

1. What is the significance of knowing your true identity in Christ in the journey of spiritual growth?

2. How does the growth of the spirit differ from the growth of the flesh?

3. Why is it essential to be certain of your spiritual rebirth before pursuing spiritual growth?

4. In the analogy of the new pilot and the old plane, how can we apply the concept of renewal to our spiritual lives?

Reflection and Application: Reflect on your journey of spiritual growth. Have you been striving to grow spiritually without first being certain of your new birth in Christ? How can you surrender to the Holy Spirit and allow Him to transform and renew your life?

Practical Exercise:

1. Prayer and Surrender: Spend time in prayer, acknowledging your need for the Holy Spirit's guidance and surrendering your flaws and weaknesses to Him.

2. Scripture Study: Meditate on passages that emphasise the believer's identity in Christ and the power of the Holy Spirit to bring transformation.

Scripture to Meditate on: Romans 8:11 - "If the Spirit of him who raised Jesus from the dead dwells in you, he who raised Christ Jesus from the dead will also give life to your mortal bodies through his Spirit who dwells in you."

As you engage with this study guide, recognise that the journey of spiritual growth involves understanding your identity in Christ and allowing the Holy Spirit to lead and renew your life. Embrace the new birth and seek to align your life with the Spirit's guidance. May you experience true transformation and maturity in your walk with God.

Understanding spirituality and the role of the flesh

Tips for Application:

1. Embrace the Union of Spirit and Flesh: Recognise that true spirituality involves the alignment of your physical body with the principles and teachings of the Holy Spirit.

2. Seek God's Presence: Strive to be filled with the Holy Spirit and allow His presence to overflow from within you, transforming your life and radiating God's nature to others.

3. Walk in Accordance with the Spirit: Live in harmony with the promptings and guidance of the Spirit, allowing the Spirit's mind to shape your thoughts and behaviours.

Study Questions:
1. What is the essence of true spirituality according to the context? How does it involve both the Spirit and the flesh?
2. How does the involvement of the physical body contribute to spirituality, as seen in the example of Jesus walking on water?
3. How does aligning our thoughts and behaviours with the teachings of the Spirit lead to maturity and spiritual development?
4. How does the pouring out of the Holy Spirit on all flesh transform believers into vessels of divine manifestation?

Reflection and Application: Reflect on your understanding of spirituality. Have you been primarily focused on the realm of the Spirit, neglecting the role of the flesh in expressing spirituality? How can you actively involve your physical body in living out spiritual principles?

Practical Exercise:
1. Prayer for Divine Presence: Spend time in prayer, inviting the Holy Spirit to fill you and overflow from within, allowing divine attributes to be expressed through your physical body.
2. Daily Application: Throughout the day, consciously seek to walk in accordance with the Spirit's guidance, aligning your thoughts and actions with His teachings.

Scripture to Meditate on: Romans 8:9 - "You, however, are not in the flesh but in the Spirit, if in fact the Spirit of God dwells in you."

As you engage with this study guide, embrace the profound transformation that occurs when your physical body becomes a vessel for expressing spirituality. Seek the presence of the Holy Spirit and allow Him to radiate God's nature through you. May you experience a deeper understanding of true spirituality and its harmonious union of spirit and flesh.

Living by the spoken word and cultivating spiritual growth

Tips for Application:

1. Seek Spiritual Nourishment: Embrace the truth that true sustenance for the physical man comes not only from physical bread but from the spoken word of God.

2. Engage with the Holy Spirit: Cultivate a lifestyle of hearing and obeying the Holy Spirit's guidance, allowing Him to impart life and understanding through the spoken word.

3. Embrace Fellowship: Recognise the significance of assembling with other believers, valuing the role of men in the body of Christ, and contributing your gifts to benefit the whole.

Study Questions:

1. What does it mean for the physical man to live not by bread alone but by every word that proceeds from the mouth of God?

2. How does engaging with the Holy Spirit and seeking the spoken word of God impact our understanding of the Scriptures?

3. Why is fellowship and unity within the body of Christ essential for spiritual growth and understanding?

Reflection and Application: Reflect on your current approach to spiritual growth and understanding of God's word. Are you actively seeking the spoken word of God through the Holy Spirit? How can you prioritise fellowship and unity within the body of Christ to enhance your spiritual journey?

Practical Exercise:

1. Prayer for Revelation: Spend time in prayer, inviting the Holy Spirit to reveal the spoken word of God to you as you engage with the Scriptures.

2. Active Participation in Fellowship: Regularly attend church gatherings and connect with other believers to contribute your gifts and receive edification.

Scripture to Meditate on: Matthew 4:4 - "But he answered, 'It is written, "Man shall not live by bread alone, but by every word that proceeds out of the mouth of God."'"

As you engage with this study guide, remember that spiritual growth and understanding come not just from reading the written word but from actively seeking the spoken word of God through the Holy Spirit. Embrace fellowship and unity within the body of Christ, allowing your gifts to contribute to the edification of others. May you experience profound transformation and a deepening of your relationship with God.

Must worship God in spirit and in truth

Tips for Application:
1. Embrace the Source of Truth: Recognise that God is the ultimate source of truth, and His Word reveals the truth that sets us free.
2. Cultivate a Relationship with Christ: Engage in a personal relationship with Jesus, accepting His teachings and submitting to His lordship.
3. Practise Truthfulness and Honesty: Embrace truthfulness and moral integrity in all aspects of your life, reflecting God's character.

Study Questions:
1. What are the key aspects of truth as revealed in Scripture?
2. Why is it important to embrace both love for what is good and hatred for evil in worshipping God in truth?
3. How does understanding and applying truth enhance our worship experience?

Reflection and Application: Reflect on how you currently approach worship and whether you have been neglecting any aspect of truth. Consider ways to integrate both love for what is good and hatred for evil into your worship.

Practical Exercise:

1. Prayer for Guidance: Seek the Holy Spirit's guidance in understanding and embracing the fullness of truth in your worship.

2. Self-Examination: Assess areas in your life where you need to cultivate truthfulness and moral integrity, and take steps to align with God's truth.

Scripture to Meditate on: John 4:24 - "God is spirit, and his worshippers must worship in the Spirit and in truth."

As you engage with this study guide, remember that worshipping God in Spirit and in truth requires an openness to the leading of the Holy Spirit and a sincere devotion that embraces both love for what is good and hatred for evil. May your worship be enriched by a deeper understanding and implementation of truth, leading to a more authentic and heartfelt devotion to God.

Abstinence from alcohol - Making room for the Holy Spirit's intoxication

Tips for Application:

1. Embrace Abstinence: Consider the benefits of abstaining from alcohol and the potential for a deeper experience with the Holy Spirit.

2. Seek Transformation: Recognize the transformative power of the Holy Spirit and desire to be filled with His wisdom, discernment, and fruits.

3. Renew Your Mindset: Shift your perspective on intoxication from a physical and temporary experience to a spiritual and lasting encounter with the Holy Spirit.

Study Questions:

1. How does alcohol's intoxication affect our mental, emotional, and physical faculties? How does it differ from the intoxication of the Holy Spirit?

2. What guidance does the Bible offer regarding alcohol consumption? How does being filled with the Holy Spirit provide an alternative form of intoxication?

3. How can you relate the concept of the soul as a cup to the idea of making room for the Holy Spirit's intoxication in your life?

Reflection and Application: Reflect on your own experiences with alcohol and its effects on your life. Consider how embracing abstinence and making room for the Holy Spirit can bring about transformation in your thought patterns, emotions, and actions.

Practical Exercise:

1. Commit to Abstinence: Make a decision to abstain from alcohol for a specific period, allowing yourself to experience a different form of intoxication through the Holy Spirit.

2. Daily Prayer for Filling: Each day, spend time in prayer, inviting the Holy Spirit to fill your soul and overflow in every aspect of your life.

Scripture to Meditate on: Ephesians 5:18 - "And do not get drunk with wine, for that is debauchery, but be filled with the Spirit."

As you engage in this study guide, may you find the strength and desire to embrace abstinence from alcohol and make room for the intoxicating presence of the Holy Spirit in your life. May His transformative power lead you to a deeper understanding of His wisdom, discernment, and love, enriching your worship and relationship with God.

Living a Supernatural Life - Understanding the difference between the Supernatural and the Spectacular

Tips for Application:

1. Prioritise the Supernatural: Seek to cultivate a deep relationship with God and make room for the constant influence of the Holy Spirit in your daily life.

2. Exercise Discernment: Differentiate between the supernatural and the spectacular. Embrace acts of obedience, love, and service as the norm in your spiritual journey, rather than pursuing extraordinary displays of power as the primary focus.

Study Questions:

1. How did Jesus exemplify a spirit-filled life, characterised by the supernatural influence of the Holy Spirit? What can we learn from His example?

2. Define the difference between the supernatural and the spectacular. Why is it essential to discern between the two in our understanding of a spiritual life?

3. What can we learn from Jesus' temptation in the wilderness about prioritising the supernatural over the spectacular in our lives?

Reflection and Application: Reflect on your own spiritual journey and the aspects that you may have been prioritising—whether the supernatural or the spectacular. How can you shift your focus to embrace the ongoing influence of the Holy Spirit in your daily life?

Practical Exercise:

1. Daily Surrender: Begin each day by surrendering your plans, desires, and actions to the leading of the Holy Spirit. Invite Him to guide and empower you throughout the day.

2. Acts of Love and Service: Identify opportunities to show love and kindness to others through acts of service, reflecting the supernatural aspect of a spirit-filled life.

Scripture to Meditate on: John 14:26 - "But the Advocate, the Holy Spirit, whom the Father will send in my name, will teach you all things and will remind you of everything I have said to you."

As you engage in this study guide, may you develop a deeper understanding of living a supernatural life, characterised by the ongoing influence of the Holy

Spirit. May you prioritise acts of obedience, love, and service, allowing the supernatural to manifest in your daily journey with God.

Study Guide: Chapter 13 – Our active engagement in the growth process

Tips for Application:

1. Yielding to the Spirit: Recognise the importance of submitting your free will to the Spirit of God, allowing Him to work through you.

2. Embrace Tests and Temptations: Instead of avoiding them, view tests and temptations as opportunities for growth and spiritual refinement.

3. Exercise Faith: Rely on God's Word and the Holy Spirit to strengthen your faith, enabling you to overcome trials and temptations.

4. Watch Your Words: Be mindful of your speech, ensuring that your confessions align with God's truth and bring life to your spirit.

5. Guard Your Heart: Seek to transform your heart and desires to align with God's will, making you less susceptible to sinful temptations.

Study Questions:

1. What role does free will play in our relationship with God? How can we actively choose to align our will with His?

2. Explain the significance of actively engaging with the process of suffering for the sake of growth and glorification. How can we apply this principle in our lives?

3. How does the process of being under tutors and governors contribute to our spiritual growth and maturity? What is the role of faith in this process?

4. How does the concept of temptation as a test challenge our perspective on trials and temptations? How can we respond with joy and resolve when facing temptations?

Reflection and Application: Reflect on your journey of faith and identify areas where you have struggled to yield your will to God's Spirit. How can you actively surrender and cooperate with His work in your life? How have you viewed tests and temptations in the past, and how can you shift your perspective to embrace them as opportunities for growth?

Practical Exercise:

1. Daily Surrender: Begin each day with a prayer of surrender, asking the Holy Spirit to guide and empower you to walk in alignment with God's will.

2. Word Confession: Practise speaking God's Word over your life, declaring truths that align with His promises and purpose for you.

3. Temptation Awareness: Be mindful of situations or areas in your life where you may be vulnerable to temptation. Seek God's help to resist and overcome these temptations.

Scripture to Meditate on: James 1:2-4 - "Consider it pure joy, my brothers and sisters, whenever you face trials of many kinds, because you know that the testing of your faith produces perseverance. Let perseverance finish its work so that you may be mature and complete, not lacking anything."

As you engage in this study guide, may you actively yield your will to the Spirit of God, embracing tests and temptations as opportunities for growth. May your faith be strengthened, and may your words align with God's truth, bringing life and transformation to your spirit. May you grow in spiritual maturity, becoming more complete and lacking in nothing, as you actively engage in the growth process with God's guidance.

Study Guide: Chapter 14 - The Hope of Eternity

Tips for Application:

1. Approach this chapter with a prayerful and open heart, seeking to understand the significance of the human body in God's plan of redemption.

2. Take notes as you read, highlighting key verses and concepts to aid in your reflection and study.

3. Engage in discussions with fellow believers to gain insights and different perspectives on the topics discussed in the chapter.

4. Apply the principles learned to your daily life, seeking to live in a way that aligns with God's purpose and plan for your life.

Study Questions:

1. What role does the human body play in God's plan for salvation?

2. How does the body of Christ serve as a covering for the spirit of Jesus? Why is this significant?

3. Explain the significance of Christ's resurrection and its relationship to our hope for eternal life.

4. How does the concept of "first fruits" tie into Christ's resurrection and the hope of our own resurrection?

5. In what ways does the falling away from the faith relate to the impending judgement and the Rapture?

Reflection and Application:

1. Reflect on the truth that our physical bodies are an essential aspect of our existence on Earth and provide us with an opportunity for salvation. How does this change the way you view and treat your body?

2. Meditate on the hope of resurrection and eternal life as you encounter challenges and difficulties in life. How can this hope sustain you during trying times?

3. Consider the urgency of the Rapture and the impending judgement. Are there areas in your life where you need to recommit to your faith and draw closer to God?

4. Take time to evaluate your spiritual journey and identify any signs of falling away from the faith. How can you actively guard against such tendencies and strengthen your relationship with God?

Practical Exercise:

1. Memorise key verses from the chapter that emphasise the hope of resurrection and the importance of Christ's sacrifice.

2. Write a prayer of thanksgiving to God for providing a way of salvation through Christ's death and resurrection.

3. Engage in a small group study or discussion with fellow believers to explore the concepts presented in this chapter further.

4. Share the message of hope and salvation with someone who may not yet know Christ, highlighting the significance of accepting Him as Saviour.

Scripture to Meditate on: 1 Corinthians 15:20-22 - "But Christ has indeed been raised from the dead, the firstfruits of those who have fallen asleep. For since death came through a man, the resurrection of the dead comes also through a man. For as in Adam all die, so in Christ all will be made alive."

www.ingramcontent.com/pod-product-compliance
Lightning Source LLC
Chambersburg PA
CBHW042125100526
44587CB00026B/4182